# BEING A BOY

# BEING A BOY

## CHARLES DUDLEY WARNER

ISBN: 978-93-90314-20-1

Published:                1897

**LECTOR HOUSE LLP**
E-MAIL: lectorpublishing@gmail.com

**FISHING ON THE SWIMMING ROCK**

*(Page 79)*

# BEING A BOY

BY

CHARLES DUDLEY WARNER

WITH ILLUSTRATIONS FROM PHOTOGRAPHS BY
CLIFTON JOHNSON

1897

# PREFACE TO THE ILLUSTRATED EDITION

This volume was first published over twenty years ago. If any of the boys described in it were real, they have long since grown up, got married, gone West, become selectmen or sheriffs, gone to Congress, invented an electric churn, become editors or preachers or commercial travelers, written a book, served a term as consul to a country the language of which they did not know, or plodded along on a farm, cultivating rheumatism and acquiring invaluable knowledge of the most fickle weather known in a region which has all the fascination and all the power of being disagreeable belonging to the most accomplished coquette in the world.

The rural life described is that of New England between 1830 and 1850, in a period of darkness, before the use of lucifer matches; but when, although religion had a touch of gloom and all pleasure was heightened by a timorous apprehension that it was sin, the sun shone, the woods were full of pungent scents, nature was strong in its invitations to cheerfulness, and girls were as sweet and winsome as they are in the old ballads.

The object of the papers composing the volume—though "object" is a strong word to use about their waywardness—was to recall scenes in the boy-life of New England, or the impressions that a boy had of that life. There was no attempt at the biography of any particular boy; the experiences given were common to the boyhood of the time and place. While the book, therefore, was not consciously biographical, it was of necessity written out of a personal knowledge. And I may be permitted to say that, as soon as I became conscious that I was dealing with a young life of the past, I tried to be faithful to it, strictly so, and to import into it nothing of later experience, either in feeling or performance. I invented nothing,—not an adventure, not a scene, not an emotion. I know from observation how difficult it is for an adult to write about childhood. Invention is apt to supply details that memory does not carry. The knowledge of the man insensibly inflates the boyhood limitations. The temptation is to make a psychological analysis of the boy's life and aspirations, and to interpret them according to the man's view of life. It seems comparatively easy to write stories about boys, and even biographies; but it is not easy to resist the temptation of inventing scenes to make them interesting, indulging in exaggerations both of adventure and of feeling which are not true to experience, inventing details impossible to be recalled by the best memory, and states of mind which are psychologically untrue to the boy's consciousness.

How far I succeeded in keeping the man out of the boy's life, my readers can judge better than the writer. The volume originally made no sensation—how could it, pitched in such a key?—but it has gone on peacefully, and, I am glad to acknowledge, has made many valuable friends. It started a brook, and a brook it has continued. In sending out this new edition with Mr. Clifton Johnson's pictures, lovingly taken from the real life and heart of New England, I may express the hope that the boy of the remote generation will lose no friends.

C. D. W.

Hartford,
May 8, 1897.

# CONTENTS

# LIST OF ILLUSTRATIONS

# BEING A BOY

## I

## BEING A BOY

One of the best things in the world to be is a boy; it requires no experience, though it needs some practice to be a good one. The disadvantage of the position is that it does not last long enough; it is soon over; just as you get used to being a boy, you have to be something else, with a good deal more work to do and not half so much fun. And yet every boy is anxious to be a man, and is very uneasy with the restrictions that are put upon him as a boy. Good fun as it is to yoke up the calves and play work, there is not a boy on a farm but would rather drive a yoke of oxen at real work. What a glorious feeling it is, indeed, when a boy is for the first time given the long whip and permitted to drive the oxen, walking by their side, swinging the long lash, and shouting "Gee, Buck!" "Haw, Golden!" "Whoa, Bright!" and all the rest of that remarkable language, until he is red in the face, and all the neighbors for half a mile are aware that something unusual is going on. If I were a boy, I am not sure but I would rather drive the oxen than have a birthday.

The proudest day of my life was one day when I rode on the neap of the cart, and drove the oxen, all alone, with a load of apples to the cider-mill. I was so little, that it was a wonder that I didn't fall off, and get under the broad wheels. Nothing could make a boy, who cared anything for his appearance, feel flatter than to be run over by the broad tire of a cart-wheel. But I never heard of one who was, and I don't believe one ever will be. As I said, it was a great day for me, but I don't remember that the oxen cared much about it. They sagged along in their great clumsy way, switching their tails in my face occasionally, and now and then giving a lurch to this or that side of the road, attracted by a choice tuft of grass. And then I "came the Julius Cæsar" over them, if you will allow me to use such a slang expression, a liberty I never should permit you. I don't know that Julius Cæsar ever drove cattle, though he must often have seen the peasants from the Campagna "haw" and "gee" them round the Forum (of course in Latin, a language that those cattle understood as well as ours do English); but what I mean is, that I stood up and "hollered" with all my might, as everybody does with oxen, as if they were born deaf, and whacked them with the long lash over the head, just as the big folks did when they drove. I think now that it was a cowardly thing to crack the patient old fellows over the face and eyes, and make them wink in their meek manner. If I am ever a boy again on a farm, I shall speak gently to the oxen, and not go screaming round the farm like a crazy man; and I shall not hit them a cruel cut with the lash every few minutes, because it looks big to do so and I cannot think of anything else to do. I never liked lickings myself, and I don't know why an ox should like them, especially as he cannot reason about the moral improvement he is to get out of them.

BEING A BOY

## THE FARM OXEN

Speaking of Latin reminds me that I once taught my cows Latin. I don't mean that I taught them to read it, for it is very difficult to teach a cow to read Latin or any of the dead languages,—a cow cares more for her cud than she does for all the classics put together. But if you begin early you can teach a cow, or a calf (if you can teach a calf anything, which I doubt), Latin as well as English. There were ten cows, which I had to escort to and from pasture night and morning. To these cows I gave the names of the Roman numerals, beginning with Unus and Duo, and going up to Decem. Decem was of course the biggest cow of the party, or at least she was the ruler of the others, and had the place of honor in the stable and everywhere else. I admire cows, and especially the exactness with which they define their social position. In this case, Decem could "lick" Novem, and Novem could "lick" Octo, and so on down to Unus, who couldn't lick anybody, except her own calf. I suppose I ought to have called the weakest cow Una instead of Unus, considering her sex; but I didn't care much to teach the cows the declensions of adjectives, in which I was not very well up myself; and besides it would be of little use to a cow. People who devote themselves too severely to study of the classics are apt to become dried up; and you should never do anything to dry up a cow. Well, these ten cows knew their names after a while, at least they appeared to, and would take their places as I called them. At least, if Octo attempted to get before Novem in going through the bars (I have heard people speak of a "pair of bars" when there were six or eight of them), or into the stable, the matter of precedence was settled then and there, and once settled there was no dispute about it afterwards. Novem either put her horns into Octo's ribs, and Octo shambled to one side, or else the two locked horns and tried the game of push and gore until one gave up. Nothing is stricter than the etiquette of a party of cows. There is nothing in royal courts equal to it; rank is exactly settled, and the same individuals always have the precedence. You know that at Windsor Castle, if the Royal Three-Ply Silver Stick should happen to get in front of the Most Royal Double-and-Twisted Golden Rod, when the court is going in to dinner, something so dreadful would happen that we don't dare to think of it. It is certain that the soup would get cold while the Golden Rod was pitching the Silver Stick out of the castle window into the moat, and perhaps the island of Great Britain itself would split in two. But the people are very careful that it never shall happen, so we shall probably never know what the effect would be. Among cows, as I say, the question is settled in short order, and in a different manner from what it sometimes is in other society. It is said that in other society there is sometimes a great scramble for the first place, for the leadership as it is called, and that women, and men too, fight for what is called position; and in order to be first they will injure their neighbors by telling stories about them and by backbiting, which is the meanest kind of biting there is, not excepting the bite of fleas. But in cow society there is nothing of this detraction in order to get the first place at the crib, or the farther stall in the stable. If the question arises, the cows turn in, horns and all, and settle it with one square fight, and that ends it. I have often admired this trait in cows.

Besides Latin, I used to try to teach the cows a little poetry, and it is a very good plan. It does not benefit the cows much, but it is excellent exercise for a boy farmer. I used to commit to memory as many short poems as I could find (the cows liked to listen to Thanatopsis about as well as anything), and repeat them when I went to the pasture, and as I drove the cows home through the sweet ferns and down the rocky slopes. It improves a boy's elocution a great deal more than driving oxen.

It is a fact, also, that if a boy repeats Thanatopsis while he is milking, that operation acquires a certain dignity.

# II

## THE BOY AS A FARMER

**AT THE PASTURE BARS**

Boys in general would be very good farmers if the current notions about farming were not so very different from those they entertain. What passes for laziness is very often an unwillingness to farm in a particular way. For instance, some morning in early summer John is told to catch the sorrel mare, harness her into the spring wagon, and put in the buffalo and the best whip, for father is obliged to drive over to the "Corners, to see a man" about some cattle, or talk with the road commissioner, or go to the store for the "women folks," and to attend to other important business; and very likely he will not be back till sundown. It must be very pressing business, for the old gentleman drives off in this way somewhere almost every pleasant day, and appears to have a great deal on his mind. Meantime, he tells John that he can play ball after he has done up the chores. As if the chores could ever be "done up" on a farm. He is first to clean out the horse-stable; then to take a bill-hook and cut down the thistles and weeds from the fence-corners in the home mowing-lot and along the road towards the village; to dig up the docks round the garden patch; to weed out the beet-bed; to hoe the early potatoes; to rake the sticks and leaves out of the front yard; in short, there is work enough laid out for John to keep him busy, it seems to him, till he comes of age; and at half an hour to sundown he is to go for the cows, and, mind he don't run 'em!

"Yes, sir," says John, "is that all?"

"Well, if you get through in good season, you might pick over those potatoes in the cellar: they are sprouting; they ain't fit to eat."

John is obliged to his father, for if there is any sort of chore more cheerful to a boy than another, on a pleasant day, it is rubbing the sprouts off potatoes in a dark cellar. And the old gentleman mounts his wagon and drives away down the enticing road, with the dog bounding along beside the wagon, and refusing to come back at John's call. John half wishes he were the dog. The dog knows the part of farming that suits him. He likes to run along the road and see all the dogs and other people, and he likes best of all to lie on the store steps at the Corners—while his master's horse is dozing at the post and his master is talking politics in the store—with the other dogs of his acquaintance, snapping at mutually annoying flies and indulging in that delightful dog gossip which is expressed by a wag of the tail and a sniff of the nose. Nobody knows how many dogs' characters are destroyed in this gossip; or how a dog may be able to insinuate suspicion by a wag of the tail as a man can by a shrug of the shoulders, or sniff a slander as a man can suggest one by raising his eyebrows.

John looks after the old gentleman driving off in state, with the odorous buffalo-robe and the new whip, and he thinks that is the sort of farming he would like to do. And he cries after his departing parent,—

"Say, father, can't I go over to the farther pasture and salt the cattle?" John knows that he could spend half a day very pleasantly in going over to that pasture, looking for bird's-nests and shying at red squirrels on the way, and who knows but he might "see" a sucker in the meadow brook, and perhaps get a "jab" at him with a sharp stick. He knows a hole where there is a whopper; and one of his plans in life is to go some day and snare him, and bring him home in triumph. It therefore is strongly impressed upon his mind that the cattle want salting. But his father, without turning his head, replies, —

"No, they don't need salting any more'n you do!" And the old equipage goes rattling down the road, and John whistles his disappointment. When I was a boy on a farm, and I suppose it is so now, cattle were never salted half enough.

**IN THE CATTLE PASTURE**

John goes to his chores, and gets through the stable as soon as he can, for that must be done; but when it comes to the outdoor work, that rather drags. There are so many things to distract the attention, — a chipmunk in the fence, a bird on a near tree, and a hen-hawk circling high in the air over the barn-yard. John loses a little time in stoning the chipmunk, which rather likes the sport, and in watching the bird to find where its nest is; and he convinces himself that he ought to watch the hawk, lest it pounce upon the chickens, and, therefore, with an easy conscience, he spends fifteen minutes in hallooing to that distant bird, and follows it away out of sight over the woods, and then wishes it would come back again. And then a carriage with two horses, and a trunk on behind, goes along the road; and there is a girl in the carriage who looks out at John, who is suddenly aware that his trousers are patched on each knee and in two places behind; and he wonders if she is rich, and whose name is on the trunk, and how much the horses cost, and whether that nice-looking man is the girl's father, and if that boy on the seat with the driver is her brother, and if he has to do chores; and as the gay sight disappears John falls to thinking about the great world beyond the farm, of cities, and people who are always dressed up, and a great many other things of which he has a very dim notion. And then a boy, whom John knows, rides by in a wagon with his father, and the boy makes a face at John, and John returns the greeting with a twist of his own visage and some symbolic gestures. All these things take time. The work of cutting down the big weeds gets on slowly, although it is not very disagreeable, or would not be if it were play. John imagines that yonder big thistle is some whiskered villain, of whom he has read in a fairy book, and he advances on him with "Die, ruffian!" and slashes off his head with the bill-hook; or he charges upon the rows of mullein-stalks as if they were rebels in regimental ranks, and hews them down without mercy. What fun it might be if there were only another boy there to help. But even war, single-handed, gets to be tiresome. It is dinner-time before John finishes the weeds, and it is cow-time before John has made much impression on the garden.

This garden John has no fondness for. He would rather hoe corn all day than work in it. Father seems to think that it is easy work that John can do, because it is near the house! John's continual plan in this life is to go fishing. When there comes a rainy day, he attempts to carry it out. But ten chances to one his father has different views. As it rains so that work cannot be done outdoors, it is a good time to work in the garden. He can run into the house during the heavy showers. John accordingly detests the garden; and the only time he works briskly in it is when he has a stent set, to do so much weeding before the Fourth of July. If he is spry he can make an extra holiday the Fourth and the day after. Two days of gunpowder and ballplaying! When I was a boy, I supposed there was some connection between such and such an amount of work done on the farm and our national freedom. I doubted if there could be any Fourth of July if my stent was not done. I, at least, worked for my Independence.

# III

# THE DELIGHTS OF FARMING

THERE are so many bright spots in the life of a farm-boy, that I sometimes think I should like to live the life over again; I should almost be willing to be a girl if it were not for the chores. There is a great comfort to a boy in the amount of work he can get rid of doing. It is sometimes astonishing how slow he can go on an errand, he who leads the school in a race. The world is new and interesting to him, and there is so much to take his attention off, when he is sent to do anything. Perhaps he couldn't explain, himself, why, when he is sent to the neighbor's after yeast, he stops to stone the frogs; he is not exactly cruel, but he wants to see if he can hit 'em. No other living thing can go so slow as a boy sent on an errand. His legs seem to be lead, unless he happens to espy a woodchuck in an adjoining lot, when he gives chase to it like a deer; and it is a curious fact about boys, that two will be a great deal slower in doing anything than one, and that the more you have to help on a piece of work the less is accomplished. Boys have a great power of helping each other to do nothing; and they are so innocent about it, and unconscious. "I went as quick as ever I could," says the boy: his father asks him why he didn't stay all night, when he has been absent three hours on a ten-minute errand. The sarcasm has no effect on the boy.

Going after the cows was a serious thing in my day. I had to climb a hill, which was covered with wild strawberries in the season. Could any boy pass by those ripe berries? And then in the fragrant hill pasture there were beds of wintergreen with red berries, tufts of columbine, roots of sassafras to be dug, and dozens of things good to eat or to smell, that I could not resist. It sometimes even lay in my way to climb a tree to look for a crow's nest, or to swing in the top, and to try if I could see the steeple of the village church. It became very important sometimes for me to see that steeple; and in the midst of my investigations the tin horn would blow a great blast from the farm-house, which would send a cold chill down my back in the hottest days. I knew what it meant. It had a frightfully impatient quaver in it, not at all like the sweet note that called us to dinner from the hayfield. It said, "Why on earth doesn't that boy come home? It is almost dark, and the cows ain't milked!" And that was the time the cows had to start into a brisk pace and make up for lost time. I wonder if any boy ever drove the cows home late, who did not say that the cows were at the very farther end of the pasture, and that "Old Brindle" was hidden in the woods, and he couldn't find her for ever so long! The brindle cow is the boy's scapegoat, many a time.

**AFTER A CROW'S NEST**

No other boy knows how to appreciate a holiday as the farm-boy does; and his best ones are of a peculiar kind. Going fishing is of course one sort. The excitement of rigging up the tackle, digging the bait, and the anticipation of great luck, — these are pure pleasures, enjoyed because they are rare. Boys who can go a-fishing any time care but little for it. Tramping all day through bush and brier, fighting flies and mosquitoes, and branches that tangle the line, and snags that break the hook, and returning home late and hungry, with wet feet and a string of speckled trout on a willow twig, and having the family crowd out at the kitchen door to look at 'em, and say, "Pretty well done for you, bub; did you catch that big one yourself?" — this is also pure happiness, the like of which the boy will never have again, not if he comes to be selectman and deacon and to "keep store."

But the holidays I recall with delight were the two days in spring and fall, when we went to the distant pasture-land, in a neighboring town, may be, to drive thither the young cattle and colts, and to bring them back again. It was a wild and rocky upland where our great pasture was, many miles from home, the road to it running by a brawling river, and up a dashing brookside among great hills. What a day's adventure it was! It was like a journey to Europe. The night before, I could scarcely sleep for thinking of it, and there was no trouble about getting me up at sunrise that morning. The breakfast was eaten, the luncheon was packed in a large basket, with bottles of root beer and a jug of switchel, which packing I superintended with the greatest interest; and then the cattle were to be collected for the march, and the horses hitched up. Did I shirk any duty? Was I slow? I think not. I was willing to run my legs off after the frisky steers, who seemed to have an idea they were going on a lark, and frolicked about, dashing into all gates, and through all bars except the right ones; and how cheerfully I did yell at them; it was a glorious chance to "holler," and I have never since heard any public speaker on the stump or at camp-meeting who could make more noise. I have often thought it fortunate that the amount of noise in a boy does not increase in proportion to his size; if it did the world could not contain it.

The whole day was full of excitement and of freedom. We were away from the farm, which to a boy is one of the best parts of farming; we saw other farms and other people at work; I had the pleasure of marching along, and swinging my whip, past boys whom I knew, who were picking up stones. Every turn of the road, every bend and rapid of the river, the great boulders by the wayside, the watering-troughs, the giant pine that had been struck by lightning, the mysterious covered bridge over the river where it was most swift and rocky and foamy, the chance eagle in the blue sky, the sense of going somewhere, — why, as I recall all these things I feel that even the Prince Imperial, as he used to dash on horseback through the Bois de Boulogne, with fifty mounted hussars clattering at his heels, and crowds of people cheering, could not have been as happy as was I, a boy in short jacket and shorter pantaloons, trudging in the dust that day behind the steers and colts, cracking my black-stock whip.

## A STRING OF SPECKLED TROUT

I wish the journey would never end; but at last, by noon, we reach the pastures and turn in the herd; and, after making the tour of the lots to make sure there are no breaks in the fences, we take our luncheon from the wagon and eat it under the trees by the spring. This is the supreme moment of the day. This is the way to live; this is like the Swiss Family Robinson, and all the rest of my delightful acquaintances in romance. Baked beans, rye-and-indian bread (moist, remember), doughnuts and cheese, pie, and root beer. What richness! You may live to dine at Delmonico's, or, if those Frenchmen do not eat each other up, at Philippe's, in the Rue Montorgueil in Paris, where the dear old Thackeray used to eat as good a dinner as anybody; but you will get there neither doughnuts, nor pie, nor root beer, nor anything so good as that luncheon at noon in the old pasture, high among the Massachusetts hills! Nor will you ever, if you live to be the oldest boy in the world, have any holiday equal to the one I have described. But I always regretted that I did not take along a fish-line, just to "throw in" the brook we passed. I know there were trout there.

# IV

## NO FARMING WITHOUT A BOY

SAY what you will about the general usefulness of boys, it is my impression
that a farm without a boy would very soon come to grief. What the boy does is
the life of the farm. He is the factotum, always in demand, always expected to do
the thousand indispensable things that nobody else will do. Upon him fall all the
odds and ends, the most difficult things. After everybody else is through, he has
to finish up. His work is like a woman's,—perpetual waiting on others. Everybody
knows how much easier it is to eat a good dinner than it is to wash the dishes
afterwards. Consider what a boy on a farm is required to do; things that must be
done, or life would actually stop.

It is understood, in the first place, that he is to do all the errands, to go to the
store, to the post-office, and to carry all sorts of messages. If he had as many legs as
a centipede, they would tire before night. His two short limbs seem to him entirely
inadequate to the task. He would like to have as many legs as a wheel has spokes,
and rotate about in the same way. This he sometimes tries to do; and people who
have seen him "turning cart-wheels" along the side of the road have supposed
that he was amusing himself, and idling his time; he was only trying to invent a
new mode of locomotion, so that he could economize his legs and do his errands
with greater dispatch. He practices standing on his head, in order to accustom
himself to any position. Leap-frog is one of his methods of getting over the ground
quickly. He would willingly go an errand any distance if he could leap-frog it with
a few other boys. He has a natural genius for combining pleasure with business.
This is the reason why, when he is sent to the spring for a pitcher of water, and the
family are waiting at the dinner-table, he is absent so long; for he stops to poke the
frog that sits on the stone, or, if there is a penstock, to put his hand over the spout
and squirt the water a little while. He is the one who spreads the grass when the
men have cut it; he mows it away in the barn; he rides the horse to cultivate the
corn, up and down the hot, weary rows; he picks up the potatoes when they are
dug; he drives the cows night and morning; he brings wood and water and splits
kindling; he gets up the horse and puts out the horse; whether he is in the house
or out of it, there is always something for him to do. Just before school in winter
he shovels paths; in summer he turns the grindstone. He knows where there are
lots of wintergreen and sweet flag root, but instead of going for them he is to stay
indoors and pare apples and stone raisins and pound something in a mortar. And
yet, with his mind full of schemes of what he would like to do, and his hands
full of occupations, he is an idle boy who has nothing to busy himself with but

school and chores! He would gladly do all the work if somebody else would do the chores, he thinks, and yet I doubt if any boy ever amounted to anything in the world, or was of much use as a man, who did not enjoy the advantages of a liberal education in the way of chores.

A boy on a farm is nothing without his pets; at least a dog, and probably rabbits, chickens, ducks, and guinea hens. A guinea hen suits a boy. It is entirely useless, and makes a more disagreeable noise than a Chinese gong. I once domesticated a young fox which a neighbor had caught. It is a mistake to suppose the fox cannot be tamed. Jacko was a very clever little animal, and behaved, in all respects, with propriety. He kept Sunday as well as any day, and all the ten commandments that he could understand. He was a very graceful playfellow, and seemed to have an affection for me. He lived in a woodpile, in the dooryard, and when I lay down at the entrance to his house and called him, he would come out and sit on his tail and lick my face just like a grown person. I taught him a great many tricks and all the virtues. That year I had a large number of hens, and Jacko went about among them with the most perfect indifference, never looking on them to lust after them, as I could see, and never touching an egg or a feather. So excellent was his reputation that I would have trusted him in the hen-roost in the dark without counting the hens. In short, he was domesticated, and I was fond of him and very proud of him, exhibiting him to all our visitors as an example of what affectionate treatment would do in subduing the brute instincts. I preferred him to my dog, whom I had, with much patience, taught to go up a long hill alone and surround the cows, and drive them home from the remote pasture. He liked the fun of it at first, but by and by he seemed to get the notion that it was a "chore," and when I whistled for him to go for the cows, he would turn tail and run the other way, and the more I whistled and threw stones at him the faster he would run. His name was Turk, and I should have sold him if he had not been the kind of dog that nobody will buy. I suppose he was not a cow-dog, but what they call a sheep-dog. At least, when he got big enough, he used to get into the pasture and chase the sheep to death. That was the way he got into trouble, and lost his valuable life. A dog is of great use on a farm, and that is the reason a boy likes him. He is good to bite peddlers and small children, and run out and yelp at wagons that pass by, and to howl all night when the moon shines. And yet, if I were a boy again, the first thing I would have should be a dog; for dogs are great companions, and as active and spry as a boy at doing nothing. They are also good to bark at woodchuck holes.

A good dog will bark at a woodchuck hole long after the animal has retired to a remote part of his residence, and escaped by another hole. This deceives the woodchuck. Some of the most delightful hours of my life have been spent in hiding and watching the hole where the dog was not. What an exquisite thrill ran through my frame when the timid nose appeared, was withdrawn, poked out again, and finally followed by the entire animal, who looked cautiously about, and then hopped away to feed on the clover. At that moment I rushed in, occupied the "home base," yelled to Turk and then danced with delight at the combat between the spunky woodchuck and the dog. They were about the same size, but science and civilization won the day. I did not reflect then that it would have been more in the interest of civilization if the woodchuck had killed the dog. I do not know why it is that boys so like to hunt and kill animals; but the excuse that I gave in this case for the murder was, that the woodchuck ate the clover and trod it down; and, in fact, was a woodchuck. It was not till long after that I learned with surprise that he is a rodent mammal, of the species *Arctomys monax*, is called at the West a ground-hog, and is eaten by people of color with great relish.

**WATCHING FOR SUNSET**

But I have forgotten my beautiful fox. Jacko continued to deport himself well until the young chickens came; he was actually cured of the fox vice of chicken-stealing. He used to go with me about the coops, pricking up his ears in an intelligent manner, and with a demure eye and the most virtuous droop of the tail. Charming fox! If he had held out a little while longer, I should have put him into a Sunday-school book. But I began to miss chickens. They disappeared mysteriously in the night. I would not suspect Jacko at first, for he looked so honest, and in the daytime he seemed to be as much interested in the chickens as I was. But one morning, when I went to call him, I found feathers at the entrance of his hole,—chicken feathers. He couldn't deny it. He was a thief. His fox nature had come out under severe temptation. And he died an unnatural death. He had a thousand virtues and one crime. But that crime struck at the foundation of society. He deceived and stole; he was a liar and a thief, and no pretty ways could hide the fact. His intelligent, bright face couldn't save him. If he had been honest, he might have grown up to be a large, ornamental fox.

# V

## THE BOY'S SUNDAY

Sunday in the New England hill towns used to begin Saturday night at sun-down; and the sun is lost to sight behind the hills there before it has set by the almanac. I remember that we used to go by the almanac Saturday night and by the visible disappearance Sunday night. On Saturday night we very slowly yielded to the influences of the holy time, which were settling down upon us, and submitted to the ablutions which were as inevitable as Sunday; but when the sun (and it never moved so slow) slid behind the hills Sunday night, the effect upon the watching boy was like a shock from a galvanic battery; something flashed through all his limbs and set them in motion, and no "play" ever seemed so sweet to him as that between sundown and dark Sunday night. This, however, was on the supposition that he had conscientiously kept Sunday, and had not gone in swimming and got drowned. This keeping of Saturday night instead of Sunday night we did not very well understand; but it seemed, on the whole, a good thing that we should rest Saturday night when we were tired, and play Sunday night when we were rested. I supposed, however, that it was an arrangement made to suit the big boys who wanted to go "courting" Sunday night. Certainly they were not to be blamed, for Sunday was the day when pretty girls were most fascinating, and I have never since seen any so lovely as those who used to sit in the gallery and in the singers' seats in the bare old meeting-houses.

Sunday to the country farmer-boy was hardly the relief that it was to the other members of the family; for the same chores must be done that day as on others, and he could not divert his mind with whistling, hand-springs, or sending the dog into the river after sticks. He had to submit, in the first place, to the restraint of shoes and stockings. He read in the Old Testament that when Moses came to holy ground he put off his shoes; but the boy was obliged to put his on, upon the holy day, not only to go to meeting, but while he sat at home. Only the emancipated country-boy, who is as agile on his bare feet as a young kid, and rejoices in the pressure of the warm soft earth, knows what a hardship it is to tie on stiff shoes. The monks who put peas in their shoes as a penance do not suffer more than the country-boy in his penitential Sunday shoes. I recall the celerity with which he used to kick them off at sundown.

Sunday morning was not an idle one for the farmer-boy. He must rise tolerably early, for the cows were to be milked and driven to pasture; family prayers were a little longer than on other days; there were the Sunday-school verses to be re-learned, for they did not stay in mind over night; perhaps the wagon was to be greased before the neighbors began to drive by; and the horse was to be caught out of the pasture, ridden home bareback, and harnessed.

**RIDING BAREBACK**

This catching the horse, perhaps two of them, was very good fun usually, and would have broken the Sunday if the horse had not been wanted for taking the family to meeting. It was so peaceful and still in the pasture on Sunday morning; but the horses were never so playful, the colts never so frisky. Round and round the lot the boy went, calling, in an entreating Sunday voice, "Jock, jock, jock, jock," and shaking his salt-dish, while the horses, with heads erect, and shaking tails and flashing heels, dashed from corner to corner, and gave the boy a pretty good race before he could coax the nose of one of them into his dish. The boy got angry, and came very near saying "dum it," but he rather enjoyed the fun, after all.

The boy remembers how his mother's anxiety was divided between the set of his turn-over collar, the parting of his hair, and his memory of the Sunday-school verses; and what a wild confusion there was through the house in getting off for meeting, and how he was kept running hither and thither, to get the hymn-book, or a palm-leaf fan, or the best whip, or to pick from the Sunday part of the garden the bunch of caraway seed. Already the deacon's mare, with a wagon load of the deacon's folks, had gone shambling past, head and tail drooping, clumsy hoofs kicking up clouds of dust, while the good deacon sat jerking the reins in an automatic way, and the "women-folks" patiently saw the dust settle upon their best summer finery. Wagon after wagon went along the sandy road, and when our boy's family started, they became part of a long procession, which sent up a mile of dust and a pungent if not pious smell of buffalo-robes. There were fiery horses in the train which had to be held in, for it was neither etiquette nor decent to pass anybody on Sunday. It was a great delight to the farmer-boy to see all this procession of horses, and to exchange sly winks with the other boys, who leaned over the wagon-seats for that purpose. Occasionally a boy rode behind, with his back to the family, and his pantomime was always something wonderful to see, and was considered very daring and wicked.

The meeting-house which our boy remembers was a high, square building, without a steeple. Within, it had a lofty pulpit, with doors underneath and closets where sacred things were kept, and where the tithing-men were supposed to imprison bad boys. The pews were square, with seats facing each other, those on one side low for the children, and all with hinges, so that they could be raised when the congregation stood up for prayers and leaned over the backs of the pews, as horses meet each other across a pasture fence. After prayers these seats used to be slammed down with a long-continued clatter, which seemed to the boys about the best part of the exercises. The galleries were very high, and the singers' seats, where the pretty girls sat, were the most conspicuous of all. To sit in the gallery, away from the family, was a privilege not often granted to the boy. The tithing-man, who carried a long rod and kept order in the house, and outdoors at noontime, sat in the gallery, and visited any boy who whispered or found curious passages in the Bible and showed them to another boy. It was an awful moment when the bushy-headed tithing-man approached a boy in sermon-time. The eyes of the whole congregation were on him, and he could feel the guilt ooze out of his burning face.

At noon was Sunday-school, and after that, before the afternoon service, in summer, the boys had a little time to eat their luncheon together at the watering-trough, where some of the elders were likely to be gathered, talking very solemnly about cattle; or they went over to a neighboring barn to see the calves; or they slipped off down the roadside to a place where they could dig sassafras or the root of the sweet flag,—roots very fragrant in the mind of many a boy with religious associations to this day. There was often an odor of sassafras in the afternoon service. It used to stand in my mind as a substitute for the Old Testament incense of the Jews. Something in the same way the big bass-viol in the choir took the place of "David's harp of solemn sound."

**TURNING THE GRINDSTONE**

The going home from meeting was more cheerful and lively than the coming to it. There was all the bustle of getting the horses out of the sheds and bringing them round to the meeting-house steps. At noon the boys sometimes sat in the wagons and swung the whips without cracking them: now it was permitted to give them a little snap in order to bring the horses up in good style; and the boy was rather proud of the horse if it pranced a little while the timid "women-folks" were trying to get in. The boy had an eye for whatever life and stir there was in a New England Sunday. He liked to drive home fast. The old house and the farm looked pleasant to him. There was an extra dinner when they reached home, and a cheerful consciousness of duty performed made it a pleasant dinner. Long before sundown the Sunday-school book had been read, and the boy sat waiting in the house with great impatience the signal that the "day of rest" was over. A boy may not be very wicked, and yet not see the need of "rest." Neither his idea of rest nor work is that of older farmers.

# VI

## THE GRINDSTONE OF LIFE

IF there is one thing more than another that hardens the lot of the farmer-boy it is the grindstone. Turning grindstones to grind scythes is one of those heroic but unobtrusive occupations for which one gets no credit. It is a hopeless kind of task, and, however faithfully the crank is turned, it is one that brings little reputation. There is a great deal of poetry about haying—I mean for those not engaged in it. One likes to hear the whetting of the scythes on a fresh morning and the response of the noisy bobolink, who always sits upon the fence and superintends the cutting of the dew-laden grass. There is a sort of music in the "swish" and a rhythm in the swing of the scythes in concert. The boy has not much time to attend to it, for it is lively business "spreading" after half a dozen men who have only to walk along and lay the grass low, while the boy has the whole hayfield on his hands. He has little time for the poetry of haying, as he struggles along, filling the air with the wet mass which he shakes over his head, and picking his way with short legs and bare feet amid the short and freshly cut stubble.

But if the scythes cut well and swing merrily it is due to the boy who turned the grindstone. Oh, it was nothing to do, just turn the grindstone a few minutes for this and that one before breakfast; any "hired man" was authorized to order the boy to turn the grindstone. How they did bear on, those great strapping fellows! Turn, turn, turn, what a weary go it was. For my part, I used to like a grindstone that "wabbled" a good deal on its axis, for when I turned it fast, it put the grinder on a lively lookout for cutting his hands, and entirely satisfied his desire that I should "turn faster." It was some sport to make the water fly and wet the grinder, suddenly starting up quickly and surprising him when I was turning very slowly. I used to wish sometimes that I could turn fast enough to make the stone fly into a dozen pieces. Steady turning is what the grinders like, and any boy who turns steadily, so as to give an even motion to the stone, will be much praised, and will be in demand. I advise any boy who desires to do this sort of work to turn steadily. If he does it by jerks and in a fitful manner, the "hired men" will be very apt to dispense with his services and turn the grindstone for each other.

This is one of the most disagreeable tasks of the boy farmer, and, hard as it is, I do not know why it is supposed to belong especially to childhood. But it is, and one of the certain marks that second childhood has come to a man on a farm is that he is asked to turn the grindstone as if he were a boy again. When the old man is good for nothing else, when he can neither mow nor pitch, and scarcely "rake after," he can turn grindstone, and it is in this way that he renews his youth. "Ain't you ashamed to have your granther turn the grindstone?" asks the hired man of the boy. So the boy takes hold and turns himself, till his little back aches. When he gets older he wishes he had replied, "Ain't you ashamed to make either an old man or a little boy do such hard grinding work?"

Doing the regular work of this world is not much, the boy thinks, but the wearisome part is the waiting on the people who do the work. And the boy is not far wrong. This is what women and boys have to do on a farm,—wait upon everybody who "works." The trouble with the boy's life is that he has no time that he can call his own. He is, like a barrel of beer, always on draught. The men-folks, having worked in the regular hours, lie down and rest, stretch themselves idly in the shade at noon, or lounge about after supper. Then the boy, who has done nothing all day but turn grindstone, and spread hay, and rake after, and run his little legs off at everybody's beck and call, is sent on some errand or some household chore, in order that time shall not hang heavy on his hands. The boy comes nearer to perpetual motion than anything else in nature, only it is not altogether a voluntary motion. The time that the farm-boy gets for his own is usually at the end of a stent. We used to be given a certain piece of corn to hoe, or a certain quantity of corn to husk in so many days. If we finished the task before the time set, we had the remainder to ourselves. In my day it used to take very sharp work to gain anything, but we were always anxious to take the chance. I think we enjoyed the holiday in anticipation quite as much as we did when we had won it. Unless it was training-day, or Fourth of July, or the circus was coming, it was a little difficult to find anything big enough to fill our anticipations of the fun we would have in the day or the two or three days we had earned. We did not want to waste the time on any common thing. Even going fishing in one of the wild mountain brooks was hardly up to the mark, for we could sometimes do that on a rainy day. Going down to the village store was not very exciting, and was on the whole a waste of our precious time. Unless we could get out our military company, life was apt to be a little blank, even on the holidays for which we had worked so hard. If you went to see another boy, he was probably at work in the hayfield or the potato-patch, and his father looked at you askance. You sometimes took hold and helped him, so that he could go and play with you; but it was usually time to go for the cows before the task was done. There has been a change, but the amusements of a boy in the country were few then. Snaring "suckers" out of the deep meadow brook used to be about as good as any that I had. The North American sucker is not an engaging animal in all respects; his body is comely enough, but his mouth is puckered up like that of a purse. The mouth is not formed for the gentle angle-worm nor the delusive fly of the fishermen. It is necessary therefore to snare the fish if you want him. In the sunny days he lies in the deep pools, by some big stone or near the bank, poising himself quite still, or only stirring his fins a little now and then, as an elephant moves his ears. He will lie so for hours,—or rather float,—in perfect idleness and apparent bliss.

The boy who also has a holiday, but cannot keep still, comes along and peeps over the bank. "Golly, ain't he a big one!" Perhaps he is eighteen inches long, and weighs two or three pounds. He lies there among his friends, little fish and big ones, quite a school of them, perhaps a district school, that only keeps in warm days in the summer. The pupils seem to have little to learn, except to balance themselves and to turn gracefully with a flirt of the tail. Not much is taught but "deportment," and some of the old suckers are perfect Turveydrops in that. The boy is armed with a pole and a stout line, and on the end of it a brass wire bent into a hoop, which is a slipnoose, and slides together when anything is caught in it. The boy approaches the bank and looks over. There he lies, calm as a whale. The boy devours him with his eyes. He is almost too much excited to drop the snare into the water without making a noise. A puff of wind comes and ruffles the surface, so that he cannot see the fish. It is calm again, and there he still is, moving his fins in peaceful security. The boy lowers his snare behind the fish and slips it along. He intends to get it around him just back of the gills and then elevate him with a sudden jerk. It is a delicate operation, for the snare will turn a little, and if it hits the fish he is off. However, it goes well, the wire is almost in place, when suddenly the fish, as if he had a warning in a dream, for he appears to see nothing, moves his tail just a little, glides out of the loop, and, with no seeming appearance of frustrating any one's plans, lounges over to the other side of the pool; and there he reposes just as if he was not spoiling the boy's holiday.

**SNARING SUCKERS**

This slight change of base on the part of the fish requires the boy to reorganize his whole campaign, get a new position on the bank, a new line of approach, and patiently wait for the wind and sun before he can lower his line. This time, cunning and patience are rewarded. The hoop encircles the unsuspecting fish. The boy's eyes almost start from his head as he gives a tremendous jerk, and feels by the dead-weight that he has got him fast. Out he comes, up he goes in the air, and the boy runs to look at him. In this transaction, however, no one can be more surprised than the sucker.

# VII

## FICTION AND SENTIMENT

THE boy farmer does not appreciate school vacations as highly as his city cousin. When school keeps he has only to "do chores and go to school," — but between terms there are a thousand things on the farm that have been left for the boy to do. Picking up stones in the pastures and piling them in heaps used to be one of them. Some lots appeared to grow stones, or else the sun every year drew them to the surface, as it coaxes the round cantelopes out of the soft garden soil; it is certain that there were fields that always gave the boys this sort of fall work. And very lively work it was on frosty mornings for the barefooted boys, who were continually turning up the larger stones in order to stand for a moment in the warm place that had been covered from the frost. A boy can stand on one leg as well as a Holland stork; and the boy who found a warm spot for the sole of his foot was likely to stand in it until the words, "Come, stir your stumps," broke in discordantly upon his meditations. For the boy is very much given to meditations. If he had his way he would do nothing in a hurry; he likes to stop and think about things, and enjoy his work as he goes along. He picks up potatoes as if each one was a lump of gold just turned out of the dirt, and requiring careful examination.

**PICKING UP POTATOES**

Although the country boy feels a little joy when school breaks up (as he does when anything breaks up, or any change takes place), since he is released from the discipline and restraint of it, yet the school is his opening into the world,—his romance. Its opportunities for enjoyment are numberless. He does not exactly know what he is set at books for; he takes spelling rather as an exercise for his lungs, standing up and shouting out the words with entire recklessness of consequences; he grapples doggedly with arithmetic and geography as something that must be cleared out of his way before recess, but not at all with the zest he would dig a woodchuck out of his hole. But recess! Was ever any enjoyment so keen as that with which a boy rushes out of the school-house door for the ten minutes of recess? He is like to burst with animal spirits; he runs like a deer; he can nearly fly; and he throws himself into play with entire self-forgetfulness, and an energy that would overturn the world if his strength were proportioned to it. For ten minutes the world is absolutely his; the weights are taken off, restraints are loosed, and he is his own master for that brief time,—as he never again will be if he lives to be as old as the king of Thule, and nobody knows how old he was. And there is the nooning, a solid hour, in which vast projects can be carried out which have been slyly matured during the school-hours; expeditions are undertaken, wars are begun between the Indians on one side and the settlers on the other, the military company is drilled (without uniforms or arms), or games are carried on which involve miles of running, and an expenditure of wind sufficient to spell the spelling-book through at the highest pitch.

**LEAP FROG AT RECESS**

Friendships are formed, too, which are fervent if not enduring, and enmities contracted which are frequently "taken out" on the spot, after a rough fashion boys have of settling as they go along; cases of long credit, either in words or trade, are not frequent with boys; boot on jack-knives must be paid on the nail; and it is considered much more honorable to out with a personal grievance at once, even if the explanation is made with the fists, than to pretend fair, and then take a sneaking revenge on some concealed opportunity. The country boy at the district school is introduced into a wider world than he knew at home, in many ways. Some big boy brings to school a copy of the Arabian Nights, a dog-eared copy, with cover, title-page, and the last leaves missing, which is passed around, and slyly read under the desk, and perhaps comes to the little boy whose parents disapprove of novel-reading, and have no work of fiction in the house except a pious fraud called "Six Months in a Convent," and the latest comic almanac. The boy's eyes dilate as he steals some of the treasures out of the wondrous pages, and he longs to lose himself in the land of enchantment open before him. He tells at home that he has seen the most wonderful book that ever was, and a big boy has promised to lend it to him. "Is it a true book, John?" asks the grandmother; "because if it isn't true, it is the worst thing that a boy can read." (This happened years ago.) John cannot answer as to the truth of the book, and so does not bring it home; but he borrows it, nevertheless, and conceals it in the barn, and lying in the hay-mow is lost in its enchantments many an odd hour when he is supposed to be doing chores. There were no chores in the Arabian Nights; the boy there had but to rub the ring and summon a genius, who would feed the calves and pick up chips and bring in wood in a minute. It was through this emblazoned portal that the boy walked into the world of books, which he soon found was larger than his own, and filled with people he longed to know.

And the farmer-boy is not without his sentiment and his secrets, though he has never been at a children's party in his life, and, in fact, never has heard that children go into society when they are seven, and give regular wine-parties when they reach the ripe age of nine. But one of his regrets at having the summer school close is dimly connected with a little girl, whom he does not care much for,—would a great deal rather play with a boy than with her at recess,—but whom he will not see again for some time,—a sweet little thing, who is very friendly with John, and with whom he has been known to exchange bits of candy wrapped up in paper, and for whom he cut in two his lead-pencil, and gave her half. At the last day of school she goes part way with John, and then he turns and goes a longer distance towards her home, so that it is late when he reaches his own. Is he late? He didn't know he was late, he came straight home when school was dismissed, only going a little way home with Alice Linton to help her carry her books. In a box in his chamber, which he has lately put a padlock on, among fish-hooks and lines and bait-boxes, odd pieces of brass, twine, early sweet apples, popcorn, beech-nuts, and other articles of value, are some little billets-doux, fancifully folded, three-cornered or otherwise, and written, I will warrant, in red or beautifully blue ink. These little notes are parting gifts at the close of school, and John, no doubt, gave his own in exchange for them, though the writing was an immense labor, and the folding was a secret bought of another boy for a big piece of sweet flag-root baked in sugar, a delicacy which John used to carry in his pantaloons pocket until his pocket was in such a state that putting his fingers into them was about as good as dipping them into the sugar-bowl at home. Each precious note contained a lock or curl of girl's hair,—a rare collection of all colors, after John had been in school many terms, and had passed through a great many parting scenes,— black, brown, red, tow-color, and some that looked like spun gold and felt like silk. The sentiment contained in the notes was that which was common in the school, and expressed a melancholy foreboding of early death, and a touching desire to leave hair enough this side the grave to constitute a sort of strand of remembrance. With little variation, the poetry that made the hair precious was in the words, and, as a Cockney would say, set to the hair, following:—

> "This lock of hair,
> Which I did wear,
> Was taken from my head;
> When this you see,
> Remember me,
> Long after I am dead."

John liked to read these verses, which always made a new and fresh impression with each lock of hair, and he was not critical; they were for him vehicles of true sentiment, and indeed they were what he used when he inclosed a clip of his own sandy hair to a friend. And it did not occur to him until he was a great deal older and less innocent to smile at them. John felt that he would sacredly keep every lock of hair intrusted to him, though death should come on the wings of cholera and take away every one of these sad, red-ink correspondents. When John's big brother one day caught sight of these treasures, and brutally told him that he "had hair enough to stuff a horse-collar," John was so outraged and shocked, as he should have been, at this rude invasion of his heart, this coarse suggestion, this profanation of his most delicate feeling, that he was only kept from crying by the resolution to "lick" his brother as soon as ever he got big enough.

# VIII

## THE COMING OF THANKSGIVING

ONE of the best things in farming is gathering the chestnuts, hickory-nuts, butternuts, and even beech-nuts, in the late fall, after the frosts have cracked the husks and the high winds have shaken them, and the colored leaves have strewn the ground. On a bright October day, when the air is full of golden sunshine, there is nothing quite so exhilarating as going nutting. Nor is the pleasure of it altogether destroyed for the boy by the consideration that he is making himself useful in obtaining supplies for the winter household. The getting-in of potatoes and corn is a different thing; that is the prose, but nutting is the poetry, of farm life. I am not sure but the boy would find it very irksome, though, if he were obliged to work at nut-gathering in order to procure food for the family. He is willing to make himself useful in his own way. The Italian boy, who works day after day at a huge pile of pine-cones, pounding and cracking them and taking out the long seeds, which are sold and eaten as we eat nuts (and which are almost as good as pumpkin-seeds, another favorite with the Italians), probably does not see the fun of nutting. Indeed, if the farmer-boy here were set at pounding off the walnut-shucks and opening the prickly chestnut-burs as a task, he would think himself an ill-used boy. What a hardship the prickles in his fingers would be! But now he digs them out with his jack-knife, and he enjoys the process, on the whole. The boy is willing to do any amount of work if it is called play.

In nutting, the squirrel is not more nimble and industrious than the boy. I like to see a crowd of boys swarm over a chestnut-grove; they leave a desert behind them like the seventeen-years locusts. To climb a tree and shake it, to club it, to strip it of its fruit and pass to the next, is the sport of a brief time. I have seen a legion of boys scamper over our grassplot under the chestnut-trees, each one as active as if he were a new patent picking-machine, sweeping the ground clean of nuts, and disappear over the hill before I could go to the door and speak to them about it. Indeed, I have noticed that boys don't care much for conversation with the owners of fruit-trees. They could speedily make their fortunes if they would work as rapidly in cotton-fields. I have never seen anything like it except a flock of turkeys removing the grasshoppers from a piece of pasture.

Perhaps it is not generally known that we get the idea of some of our best military manoeuvres from the turkey. The deploying of the skirmish-line in advance of an army is one of them. The drum-major of our holiday militia companies is copied exactly from the turkey gobbler; he has the same splendid appearance, the same proud step, and the same martial aspect. The gobbler does not lead his forces in the field, but goes behind them, like the colonel of a regiment, so that he can see every part of the line and direct its movements. This resemblance is one of the most singular things in natural history. I like to watch the gobbler manoeuvring his forces in a grasshopper-field. He throws out his company of two dozen turkeys in a crescent-shaped skirmish-line, the number disposed at equal distances, while he walks majestically in the rear. They advance rapidly, picking right and left, with military precision, killing the foe and disposing of the dead bodies with the same peck. Nobody has yet discovered how many grasshoppers a turkey will hold; but he is very much like a boy at a Thanksgiving dinner,—he keeps on eating as long as the supplies last.

## POUNDING OFF SHUCKS

The gobbler, in one of these raids, does not condescend to grab a single grass-hopper,—at least, not while anybody is watching him. But I suppose he makes up for it when his dignity cannot be injured by having spectators of his voracity; perhaps he falls upon the grasshoppers when they are driven into a corner of the field. But he is only fattening himself for destruction; like all greedy persons, he comes to a bad end. And if the turkeys had any Sunday-school, they would be taught this.

The New England boy used to look forward to Thanksgiving as the great event of the year. He was apt to get stents set him,—so much corn to husk, for instance, before that day, so that he could have an extra play-spell; and in order to gain a day or two, he would work at his task with the rapidity of half a dozen boys. He had the day after Thanksgiving always as a holiday, and this was the day he counted on. Thanksgiving itself was rather an awful festival,—very much like

Sunday, except for the enormous dinner, which filled his imagination for months before as completely as it did his stomach for that day and a week after. There was an impression in the house that that dinner was the most important event since the landing from the Mayflower. Heliogabalus, who did not resemble a Pilgrim Father at all, but who had prepared for himself in his day some very sumptuous banquets in Rome, and ate a great deal of the best he could get (and liked peacocks stuffed with asafoetida, for one thing), never had anything like a Thanksgiving dinner; for do you suppose that he, or Sardanapalus either, ever had twenty-four different kinds of pie at one dinner? Therein many a New England boy is greater than the Roman emperor or the Assyrian king, and these were among the most luxurious eaters of their day and generation. But something more is necessary to make good men than plenty to eat, as Heliogabalus no doubt found when his head was cut off. Cutting off the head was a mode the people had of expressing disapproval of their conspicuous men. Nowadays they elect them to a higher office, or give them a mission to some foreign country, if they do not do well where they are.

For days and days before Thanksgiving the boy was kept at work evenings, pounding and paring and cutting up and mixing (not being allowed to taste much), until the world seemed to him to be made of fragrant spices, green fruit, raisins, and pastry,—a world that he was only yet allowed to enjoy through his nose. How filled the house was with the most delicious smells! The mince-pies that were made! If John had been shut in solid walls with them piled about him, he couldn't have eaten his way out in four weeks. There were dainties enough cooked in those two weeks to have made the entire year luscious with good living, if they had been scattered along in it. But people were probably all the better for scrimping themselves a little in order to make this a great feast. And it was not by any means over in a day. There were weeks deep of chicken-pie and other pastry. The cold buttery was a cave of Aladdin, and it took a long time to excavate all its riches.

Thanksgiving Day itself was a heavy day, the hilarity of it being so subdued by going to meeting, and the universal wearing of the Sunday clothes, that the boy couldn't see it. But if he felt little exhilaration, he ate a great deal. The next day was the real holiday. Then were the merry-making parties, and perhaps the skatings and sleighrides, for the freezing weather came before the governor's proclamation in many parts of New England. The night after Thanksgiving occurred, perhaps, the first real party that the boy had ever attended, with live girls in it, dressed so bewitchingly. And there he heard those philandering songs, and played those sweet games of forfeits, which put him quite beside himself, and kept him awake that night till the rooster crowed at the end of his first chicken-nap. What a new world did that party open to him! I think it likely that he saw there, and probably did not dare say ten words to, some tall, graceful girl, much older than himself, who seemed to him like a new order of being. He could see her face just as plainly in the darkness of his chamber. He wondered if she noticed how awkward he was, and how short his trousers-legs were. He blushed as he thought of his rather ill-fitting shoes; and determined, then and there, that he wouldn't be put off with a ribbon any longer, but would have a young man's necktie. It was somewhat painful thinking the party over, but it was delicious too. He did not think, probably, that he would die for that tall, handsome girl; he did not put it exactly in that way. But he rather resolved to live for her, — which might in the end amount to the same thing. At least, he thought that nobody would live to speak twice disrespectfully of her in his presence.

# IX

## THE SEASON OF PUMPKIN-PIE

WHAT John said was, that he didn't care much for pumpkin-pie; but that was after he had eaten a whole one. It seemed to him then that mince would be better.

The feeling of a boy towards pumpkin-pie has never been properly considered. There is an air of festivity about its approach in the fall. The boy is willing to help pare and cut up the pumpkin, and he watches with the greatest interest the stirring-up process and the pouring into the scalloped crust. When the sweet savor of the baking reaches his nostrils, he is filled with the most delightful anticipations. Why should he not be? He knows that for months to come the buttery will contain golden treasures, and that it will require only a slight ingenuity to get at them.

The fact is, that the boy is as good in the buttery as in any part of farming. His elders say that the boy is always hungry; but that is a very coarse way to put it. He has only recently come into a world that is full of good things to eat, and there is on the whole a very short time in which to eat them; at least he is told, among the first information he receives, that life is short. Life being brief, and pie and the like fleeting, he very soon decides upon an active campaign. It may be an old story to people who have been eating for forty or fifty years, but it is different with a beginner. He takes the thick and thin as it comes, as to pie, for instance. Some people do make them very thin. I knew a place where they were not thicker than the poor man's plaster; they were spread so thin upon the crust that they were better fitted to draw out hunger than to satisfy it. They used to be made up by the great oven-full and kept in the dry cellar, where they hardened and dried to a toughness you would hardly believe. This was a long time ago, and they make the pumpkin-pie in the country better now, or the race of boys would have been so discouraged that I think they would have stopped coming into the world.

The truth is, that boys have always been so plenty that they are not half appreciated. We have shown that a farm could not get along without them, and yet their rights are seldom recognized. One of the most amusing things is their effort to acquire personal property. The boy has the care of the calves; they always need feeding or shutting up or letting out; when the boy wants to play, there are those calves to be looked after,—until he gets to hate the name of calf. But in consideration of his faithfulness, two of them are given to him. There is no doubt that they are his; he has the entire charge of them. When they get to be steers, he spends all his holidays in breaking them in to a yoke. He gets them so broken in that they will run like a pair of deer all over the farm, turning the yoke, and kicking their heels, while he follows in full chase, shouting the ox language till he is red in the face. When the steers grow up to be cattle, a drover one day comes along and takes them away, and the boy is told that he can have another pair of calves; and so, with undiminished faith, he goes back and begins over again to make his fortune. He owns lambs and young colts in the same way, and makes just as much out of them.

There are ways in which the farmer-boy can earn money, as by gathering the early chestnuts and taking them to the Corner store, or by finding turkeys' eggs and selling them to his mother; and another way is to go without butter at the table,—but the money thus made is for the heathen. John read in Dr. Livingstone that some of the tribes in Central Africa (which is represented by a blank spot in the atlas) use the butter to grease their hair, putting on pounds of it at a time; and he said he had rather eat his butter than have it put to that use, especially as it melted away so fast in that hot climate.

Of course it was explained to John that the missionaries do not actually carry butter to Africa, and that they must usually go without it themselves there, it being almost impossible to make it good from the milk in the cocoanuts. And it was further explained to him that, even if the heathen never received his butter or the money for it, it was an excellent thing for a boy to cultivate the habit of self-denial and of benevolence, and if the heathen never heard of him he would be blessed for his generosity. This was all true.

But John said that he was tired of supporting the heathen out of his butter, and he wished the rest of the family would also stop eating butter and save the money for missions; and he wanted to know where the other members of the family got their money to send to the heathen; and his mother said that he was about half right, and that self-denial was just as good for grown people as it was for little boys and girls.

The boy is not always slow to take what he considers his rights. Speaking of those thin pumpkin-pies kept in the cellar cupboard, I used to know a boy who afterwards grew to be a selectman, and brushed his hair straight up like General Jackson, and went to the legislature, where he always voted against every measure that was proposed, in the most honest manner, and got the reputation of being the "watch-dog of the treasury." Rats in the cellar were nothing to be compared to this boy for destructiveness in pies. He used to go down, whenever he could make an excuse, to get apples for the family, or draw a mug of cider for his dear old grandfather (who was a famous story-teller about the Revolutionary War, and would no doubt have been wounded in battle if he had not been as prudent as he was patriotic), and come up stairs with a tallow candle in one hand and the apples or cider in the other, looking as innocent and as unconscious as if he had never done anything in his life except deny himself butter for the sake of the heathen. And yet this boy would have buttoned under his jacket an entire round pumpkin-pie. And the pie was so well made and so dry that it was not injured in the least, and it never hurt the boy's clothes a bit more than if it had been inside of him instead of outside; and this boy would retire to a secluded place and eat it with another boy, being never suspected, because he was not in the cellar long enough to eat a pie, and he never appeared to have one about him. But he did something worse than this. When his mother saw that pie after pie departed, she told the family that she suspected the hired man; and the boy never said a word, which was the meanest kind of lying. That hired man was probably regarded with suspicion by the family to the end of his days, and if he had been accused of robbing they would have believed him guilty.

I shouldn't wonder if that selectman occasionally has remorse now about that pie; dreams, perhaps, that it is buttoned up under his jacket and sticking to him like a breastplate; that it lies upon his stomach like a round and red-hot nightmare, eating into his vitals. Perhaps not. It is difficult to say exactly what was the sin of stealing that kind of pie, especially if the one who stole it ate it. It could have been used for the game of pitching quoits, and a pair of them would have made very fair wheels for the dog-cart. And yet it is probably as wrong to steal a thin pie as a thick one; and it made no difference because it was easy to steal this sort. Easy stealing is no better than easy lying, where detection of the lie is difficult. The boy who steals his mother's pies has no right to be surprised when some other boy steals his watermelons. Stealing is like charity in one respect, — it is apt to begin at home.

# X

## FIRST EXPERIENCE OF THE WORLD

IF I were forced to be a boy, and a boy in the country,—the best kind of boy to be in the summer,—I would be about ten years of age. As soon as I got any older, I would quit it. The trouble with a boy is that just as he begins to enjoy himself he is too old, and has to be set to doing something else. If a country boy were wise he would stay at just that age when he could enjoy himself most, and have the least expected of him in the way of work.

Of course the perfectly good boy will always prefer to work, and to do "chores" for his father and errands for his mother and sisters, rather than enjoy himself in his own way. I never saw but one such boy. He lived in the town of Goshen,—not the place where the butter is made, but a much better Goshen than that. And I never saw *him*, but I heard of him; and being about the same age, as I supposed, I was taken once from Zoar, where I lived, to Goshen to see him. But he was dead. He had been dead almost a year, so that it was impossible to see him. He died of the most singular disease: it was from *not* eating green apples in the season of them. This boy, whose name was Solomon, before he died would rather split up kindling-wood for his mother than go a-fishing: the consequence was, that he was kept at splitting kindling-wood and such work most of the time, and grew a better and more useful boy day by day. Solomon would not disobey his parents and eat green apples,—not even when they were ripe enough to knock off with a stick,— but he had such a longing for them that he pined and passed away. If he had eaten the green apples he would have died of them, probably; so that his example is a difficult one to follow. In fact, a boy is a hard subject to get a moral from. All his little playmates who ate green apples came to Solomon's funeral, and were very sorry for what they had done.

John was a very different boy from Solomon, not half so good, nor half so dead. He was a farmer's boy, as Solomon was, but he did not take so much interest in the farm. If John could have had his way he would have discovered a cave full of diamonds, and lots of nail-kegs full of gold-pieces and Spanish dollars, with a pretty little girl living in the cave, and two beautifully caparisoned horses, upon which, taking the jewels and money, they would have ridden off together, he did not know where. John had got thus far in his studies, which were apparently arithmetic and geography, but were in reality the Arabian Nights, and other books of high and mighty adventure. He was a simple country boy, and did not know much about the world as it is, but he had one of his own imagination, in which he lived a good deal. I dare say he found out soon enough what the world is, and he had a lesson or two when he was quite young, in two incidents, which I may as well relate.

## RUNNING ON THE STONE WALL

If you had seen John at this time, you might have thought he was only a shabbily dressed country lad, and you never would have guessed what beautiful thoughts he sometimes had as he went stubbing his toes along the dusty road, nor what a chivalrous little fellow he was. You would have seen a short boy, barefooted, with trousers at once too big and too short, held up, perhaps, by one suspender only; a checked cotton shirt; and a hat of braided palm-leaf, frayed at the edges and bulged up in the crown. It is impossible to keep a hat neat if you use it to catch bumble-bees and whisk 'em; to bail the water from a leaky boat; to catch minnows in; to put over honey-bees' nests; and to transport pebbles, strawberries, and hens' eggs. John usually carried a sling in his hand, or a bow, or a limber stick sharp at one end, from which he could sling apples a great distance. If he walked in the road, he walked in the middle of it, shuffling up the dust; or, if he went elsewhere, he was likely to be running on the top of the fence or the stone-wall, and chasing chipmunks.

John knew the best place to dig sweet-flag in all the farm; it was in a meadow by the river, where the bobolinks sang so gayly. He never liked to hear the bobolink sing, however, for he said it always reminded him of the whetting of a scythe, and *that* reminded him of spreading hay; and if there was anything he hated it was spreading hay after the mowers. "I guess you wouldn't like it yourself," said John, "with the stubs getting into your feet, and the hot sun, and the men getting ahead of you, all you could do."

Towards evening once, John was coming along the road home with some stalks of the sweet-flag in his hand; there is a succulent pith in the end of the stalk which is very good to eat, tender, and not so strong as the root; and John liked to pull it, and carry home what he did not eat on the way. As he was walking along he met a carriage, which stopped opposite to him; he also stopped and bowed, as country boys used to bow in John's day. A lady leaned from the carriage and said,—

"What have you got, little boy?"

She seemed to be the most beautiful woman John had ever seen; with light hair, dark, tender eyes, and the sweetest smile. There was that in her gracious mien and in her dress which reminded John of the beautiful castle ladies, with whom he was well acquainted in books. He felt that he knew her at once, and he also seemed to be a sort of young prince himself. I fancy he didn't look much like one. But of his own appearance he thought not at all, as he replied to the lady's question, without the least embarrassment,—

"It's sweet-flag stalk; would you like some?"

"Indeed, I should like to taste it," said the lady, with a most winning smile. "I used to be very fond of it when I was a little girl."

John was delighted that the lady should like sweet-flag, and that she was pleased to accept it from him. He thought himself that it was about the best thing to eat he knew. He handed up a large bunch of it. The lady took two or three stalks, and was about to return the rest, when John said,—

"Please keep it all, ma'am. I can get lots more. I know where it's ever so thick."

"Thank you, thank you," said the lady; and as the carriage started she reached out her hand to John. He did not understand the motion, until he saw a cent drop in the road at his feet. Instantly all his illusion and his pleasure vanished. Something like tears were in his eyes as he shouted,—

"I don't want your cent. I don't sell flag!"

John was intensely mortified. "I suppose," he said, "she thought I was a sort of beggar-boy. To think of selling flag!"

At any rate, he walked away and left the cent in the road, a humiliated boy. The next day he told Jim Gates about it. Jim said he was green not to take the money; he'd go and look for it now, if he would tell him about where it dropped. And Jim did spend an hour poking about in the dirt, but he did not find the cent. Jim, however, had an idea: he said he was going to dig sweet-flag, and see if another carriage wouldn't come along.

John's next rebuff and knowledge of the world was of another sort. He was again walking the road at twilight, when he was overtaken by a wagon with one seat, upon which were two pretty girls, and a young gentleman sat between them driving. It was a merry party, and John could hear them laughing and singing as they approached him. The wagon stopped when it overtook him, and one of the sweet-faced girls leaned from the seat and said, quite seriously and pleasantly,—

"Little boy, how's your mar?"

John was surprised and puzzled for a moment. He had never seen the young lady, but he thought that she perhaps knew his mother; at any rate his instinct of politeness made him say, —

"She's pretty well, I thank you."

"Does she know you are out?"

And thereupon all three in the wagon burst into a roar of laughter and dashed on.

It flashed upon John in a moment that he had been imposed on, and it hurt him dreadfully. His self-respect was injured somehow, and he felt as if his lovely, gentle mother had been insulted. He would like to have thrown a stone at the wagon, and in a rage he cried, —

"You're a nice" —But he couldn't think of any hard, bitter words quick enough.

Probably the young lady, who might have been almost any young lady, never knew what a cruel thing she had done.

# XI

## HOME INVENTIONS

THE winter season is not all sliding down hill for the farmer-boy by any means; yet he contrives to get as much fun out of it as from any part of the year. There is a difference in boys: some are always jolly, and some go scowling always through life as if they had a stone-bruise on each heel. I like a jolly boy.

I used to know one who came round every morning to sell molasses candy, offering two sticks for a cent apiece; it was worth fifty cents a day to see his cheery face. That boy rose in the world. He is now the owner of a large town at the West. To be sure, there are no houses in it except his own; but there is a map of it and roads and streets are laid out on it, with dwellings and churches and academies and a college and an opera-house, and you could scarcely tell it from Springfield or Hartford, on paper. He and all his family have the fever and ague, and shake worse than the people at Lebanon: but they do not mind it; it makes them lively, in fact. Ed May is just as jolly as he used to be. He calls his town Mayopolis, and expects to be mayor of it; his wife, however, calls the town Maybe.

**COASTING**

The farmer-boy likes to have winter come, for one thing, because it freezes up the ground so that he can't dig in it; and it is covered with snow, so that there is no picking up stones, nor driving the cows to pasture. He would have a very easy time if it were not for the getting up before daylight to build the fires and do the "chores." Nature intended the long winter nights for the farmer-boy to sleep; but in my day he was expected to open his sleepy eyes when the cock crew, get out of the warm bed and light a candle, struggle into his cold pantaloons, and pull on boots in which the thermometer would have gone down to zero, rake open the coals on the hearth and start the morning fire, and then go to the barn to "fodder." The frost was thick on the kitchen windows; the snow was drifted against the door; and the journey to the barn, in the pale light of dawn, over the creaking snow, was like an exile's trip to Siberia. The boy was not half awake when he stumbled into the cold barn, and was greeted by the lowing and bleating and neighing of cattle waiting for their breakfast. How their breath steamed up from the mangers, and hung in frosty spears from their noses! Through the great lofts above the hay, where the swallows nested, the winter wind whistled and the snow sifted. Those old barns were well ventilated.

I used to spend much valuable time in planning a barn that should be tight and warm, with a fire in it if necessary in order to keep the temperature somewhere near the freezing point. I couldn't see how the cattle could live in a place where a lively boy, full of young blood, would freeze to death in a short time if he did not swing his arms and slap his hands, and jump about like a goat. I thought I would have a sort of perpetual manger that should shake down the hay when it was wanted, and a self-acting machine that should cut up the turnips and pass them into the mangers, and water always flowing for the cattle and horses to drink. With these simple arrangements I could lie in bed, and know that the "chores" were doing themselves. It would also be necessary, in order that I should not be disturbed, that the crow should be taken out of the roosters, but I could think of no process to do it. It seems to me that the hen-breeders, if they know as much as they say they do, might raise a breed of crowless roosters, for the benefit of boys, quiet neighborhoods, and sleepy families.

There was another notion that I had, about kindling the kitchen fire, that I never carried out. It was, to have a spring at the head of my bed, connecting with a wire, which should run to a torpedo which I would plant overnight in the ashes of the fireplace. By touching the spring I could explode the torpedo, which would scatter the ashes and uncover the live coals, and at the same time shake down the sticks of wood which were standing by the side of the ashes in the chimney, and the fire would kindle itself. This ingenious plan was frowned on by the whole family, who said they did not want to be waked up every morning by an explosion. And yet they expected me to wake up without an explosion. A boy's plans for making life agreeable are hardly ever heeded.

I never knew a boy farmer who was not eager to go to the district school in the winter. There is such a chance for learning, that he must be a dull boy who does not come out in the spring a fair skater, an accurate snowballer, and an accomplished slider downhill, with or without a board, on his seat, on his stomach, or on his feet.

Take a moderate hill, with a foot-slide down it worn to icy smoothness, and a "go-round" of boys on it, and there is nothing like it for whittling away boot-leather. The boy is the shoemaker's friend. An active lad can wear down a pair of cowhide soles in a week so that the ice will scrape his toes. Sledding or coasting is also slow fun compared to the "bareback" sliding down a steep hill over a hard, glistening crust. It is not only dangerous, but it is destructive to jacket and pantaloons to a degree to make a tailor laugh. If any other animal wore out his skin as fast as a schoolboy wears out his clothes in winter, it would need a new one once a month. In a country district-school, patches were not by any means a sign of poverty, but of the boy's courage and adventurous disposition. Our elders used to threaten to dress us in leather and put sheet-iron seats in our trousers. The boy *said* that he wore out his trousers on the hard seats in the school-house ciphering hard sums. For that extraordinary statement he received two castigations,—one at home, that was mild, and one from the schoolmaster, who was careful to lay the rod upon the boy's sliding-place, punishing him, as he jocosely called it, on a sliding scale, according to the thinness of his pantaloons.

What I liked best at school, however, was the study of history, early history, the Indian wars. We studied it mostly at noontime, and we had it illustrated as the children nowadays have "object-lessons,"—though our object was not so much to have lessons as it was to revive real history.

Back of the school-house rose a round hill, upon which tradition said had stood in colonial times a block-house, built by the settlers for defense against the Indians. For the Indians had the idea that the whites were not settled enough, and used to come nights to settle them with a tomahawk. It was called Fort Hill. It was very steep on each side, and the river ran close by. It was a charming place in summer, where one could find laurel, and checkerberries, and sassafras roots, and sit in the cool breeze, looking at the mountains across the river, and listening to the murmur of the Deerfield. The Methodists built a meeting-house there afterwards, but the hill was so slippery in winter that the aged could not climb it, and the wind raged so fiercely that it blew nearly all the young Methodists away (many of whom were afterwards heard of in the West), and finally the meeting-house itself came down into the valley and grew a steeple, and enjoyed itself ever afterwards. It used to be a notion in New England that a meeting-house ought to stand as near heaven as possible.

The boys at our school divided themselves into two parties; one was the Early Settlers and the other the Pequots, the latter the most numerous. The Early Settlers built a snow fort on the hill, and a strong fortress it was, constructed of snowballs rolled up to a vast size (larger than the Cyclopean blocks of stone which form the ancient Etruscan walls in Italy), piled one upon another, and the whole cemented by pouring on water which froze and made the walls solid. The Pequots helped the whites build it. It had a covered way under the snow, through which only could it be entered, and it had bastions and towers and openings to fire from, and a great many other things for which there are no names in military books. And it had a glacis and a ditch outside.

## IN SCHOOL

When it was completed, the Early Settlers, leaving the women in the school-house, a prey to the Indians, used to retire into it, and await the attack of the Pequots. There was only a handful of the garrison, while the Indians were many, and also barbarous. It was agreed that they should be barbarous. And it was in this light that the great question was settled whether a boy might snowball with balls that he had soaked over night in water and let freeze. They were as hard as cobblestones, and if a boy should be hit in the head by one of them he could not tell whether he was a Pequot or an Early Settler. It was considered as unfair to use these ice-balls in an open fight, as it is to use poisoned ammunition in real war. But as the whites were protected by the fort, and the Indians were treacherous by nature, it was decided that the latter might use the hard missiles.

The Pequots used to come swarming up the hill, with hideous war-whoops, attacking the fort on all sides with great noise and a shower of balls. The garrison replied with yells of defiance and well-directed shots, hurling back the invaders when they attempted to scale the walls. The Settlers had the advantage of position, but they were sometimes overpowered by numbers, and would often have had to surrender but for the ringing of the school-bell. The Pequots were in great fear of the school-bell.

I do not remember that the whites ever hauled down their flag and surrendered voluntarily; but once or twice the fort was carried by storm and the garrison were massacred to a boy, and thrown out of the fortress, having been first scalped. To take a boy's cap was to scalp him, and after that he was dead, if he played fair. There were a great many hard hits given and taken, but always cheerfully, for it was in the cause of our early history. The history of Greece and Rome was stuff compared to this. And we had many boys in our school who could imitate the Indian war-whoop enough better than they could scan *arma, virumque cano*.

# XII

## THE LONELY FARM-HOUSE

THE winter evenings of the farmer-boy in New England used not to be so gay as to tire him of the pleasures of life before he became of age. A remote farm-house, standing a little off the road, banked up with sawdust and earth to keep the frost out of the cellar, blockaded with snow, and flying a blue flag of smoke from its chimney, looks like a besieged fort. On cold and stormy winter nights, to the traveler wearily dragging along in his creaking sleigh, the light from its windows suggests a house of refuge and the cheer of a blazing fire. But it is no less a fort, into which the family retire when the New England winter on the hills really sets in.

The boy is an important part of the garrison. He is not only one of the best means of communicating with the outer world, but he furnishes half the entertainment and takes two thirds of the scolding of the family circle. A farm would come to grief without a boy on it, but it is impossible to think of a farm-house without a boy in it.

**A REMOTE FARM-HOUSE**

"That boy" brings life into the house; his tracks are to be seen everywhere, he leaves all the doors open, he hasn't half filled the wood-box, he makes noise enough to wake the dead; or he is in a brown-study by the fire and cannot be stirred, or he has fastened a grip upon some Crusoe book which cannot easily be shaken off. I suppose that the farmer-boy's evenings are not now what they used to be; that he has more books, and less to do, and is not half so good a boy as formerly, when he used to think the almanac was pretty lively reading, and the comic almanac, if he could get hold of that, was a supreme delight.

Of course he had the evenings to himself after he had done the "chores" at the barn, brought in the wood and piled it high in the box, ready to be heaped upon the great open fire. It was nearly dark when he came from school (with its continuation of snowballing and sliding), and he always had an agreeable time stumbling and fumbling around in barn and woodhouse in the waning light.

John used to say that he supposed nobody would do his "chores" if he did not get home till midnight; and he was never contradicted. Whatever happened to him, and whatever length of days or sort of weather was produced by the almanac, the cardinal rule was that he should be at home before dark.

John used to imagine what people did in the dark ages, and wonder sometimes whether he wasn't still in them.

Of course, John had nothing to do all the evening, after his "chores,"—except little things. While he drew his chair up to the table in order to get the full radiance of the tallow candle on his slate or his book, the women of the house also sat by the table knitting and sewing. The head of the house sat in his chair, tipped back against the chimney; the hired man was in danger of burning his boots in the fire. John might be deep in the excitement of a bear story, or be hard at writing a "composition" on his greasy slate; but, whatever he was doing, he was the only one who could always be interrupted. It was he who must snuff the candles, and put on a stick of wood, and toast the cheese, and turn the apples, and crack the nuts. He knew where the fox-and-geese board was, and he could find the twelve-men-Morris. Considering that he was expected to go to bed at eight o'clock, one would say that the opportunity for study was not great, and that his reading was rather interrupted. There seemed to be always something for him to do, even when all the rest of the family came as near being idle as is ever possible in a New England household.

No wonder that John was not sleepy at eight o'clock: he had been flying about while the others had been yawning before the fire. He would like to sit up just to see how much more solemn and stupid it would become as the night went on; he wanted to tinker his skates, to mend his sled, to finish that chapter. Why should he go away from that bright blaze, and the company that sat in its radiance, to the cold and solitude of his chamber? Why didn't the people who were sleepy go to bed?

How lonesome the old house was; how cold it was, away from that great central fire in the heart of it; how its timbers creaked as if in the contracting pinch of the frost; what a rattling there was of windows, what a concerted attack upon the clapboards; how the floors squeaked, and what gusts from round corners came to snatch the feeble flame of the candle from the boy's hand! How he shivered, as he paused at the staircase window to look out upon the great fields of snow, upon the stripped forest, through which he could hear the wind raving in a kind of fury, and up at the black flying clouds, amid which the young moon was dashing and driven on like a frail shallop at sea! And his teeth chattered more than ever when he got into the icy sheets, and drew himself up into a ball in his flannel nightgown, like a fox in his hole.

For a little time he could hear the noises downstairs, and an occasional laugh; he could guess that now they were having cider, and now apples were going round; and he could feel the wind tugging at the house, even sometimes shaking the bed. But this did not last long. He soon went away into a country he always delighted to be in; a calm place where the wind never blew, and no one dictated the time of going to bed to any one else. I like to think of him sleeping there, in such rude surroundings, ingenuous, innocent, mischievous, with no thought of the buffeting he is to get from a world that has a good many worse places for a boy than the hearth of an old farm-house, and the sweet though undemonstrative affection of its family life.

But there were other evenings in the boy's life that were different from these at home, and one of them he will never forget. It opened a new world to John, and set him into a great flutter. It produced a revolution in his mind in regard to neckties; it made him wonder if greased boots were quite the thing compared with blacked boots; and he wished he had a long looking-glass, so that he could see, as he walked away from it, what was the effect of round patches on the portion of his trousers he could not see except in a mirror; and if patches were quite stylish, even on everyday trousers. And he began to be very much troubled about the parting of his hair, and how to find out on which side was the natural part.

The evening to which I refer was that of John's first party. He knew the girls at school, and he was interested in some of them with a different interest from that he took in the boys. He never wanted to "take it out" with one of them, for an insult, in a stand-up fight, and he instinctively softened a boy's natural rudeness when he was with them. He would help a timid little girl to stand erect and slide; he would draw her on his sled, till his hands were stiff with cold, without a murmur; he would generously give her red apples into which he longed to set his own sharp teeth; and he would cut in two his lead-pencil for a girl, when he would not for a boy. Had he not some of the beautiful auburn tresses of Cynthia Rudd in his skate, spruce-gum, and wintergreen box at home? And yet the grand sentiment of life was little awakened in John. He liked best to be with boys, and their rough play suited him better than the amusements of the shrinking, fluttering, timid, and sensitive little girls. John had not learned then that a spider-web is stronger than a cable; or that a pretty little girl could turn him round her finger a great deal easier than a big bully of a boy could make him cry "enough."

John had indeed been at spelling-schools, and had accomplished the feat of "going home with a girl" afterwards; and he had been growing into the habit of looking around in meeting on Sunday, and noticing how Cynthia was dressed, and not enjoying the service quite as much if Cynthia was absent as when she was present. But there was very little sentiment in all this, and nothing whatever to make John blush at hearing her name.

But now John was invited to a regular party. There was the invitation, in a three-cornered billet, sealed with a transparent wafer: "Miss C. Rudd requests the pleasure of the company of," etc., all in blue ink, and the finest kind of pin-scratching writing. What a precious document it was to John! It even exhaled a faint sort of perfume, whether of lavender or caraway-seed he could not tell. He read it over a hundred times, and showed it confidentially to his favorite cousin, who had beaux of her own, and had even "sat up" with them in the parlor. And from this sympathetic cousin John got advice as to what he should wear and how he should conduct himself at the party.

# XIII

## JOHN'S FIRST PARTY

Iт turned out that John did not go after all to Cynthia Rudd's party, having broken through the ice on the river when he was skating that day, and, as the boy who pulled him out said, "come within an inch of his life." But he took care not to tumble into anything that should keep him from the next party, which was given with due formality by Melinda Mayhew.

John had been many a time to the house of Deacon Mayhew, and never with any hesitation, even if he knew that both the deacon's daughters—Melinda and Sophronia—were at home. The only fear he had felt was of the deacon's big dog, who always surlily watched him as he came up the tanbark walk, and made a rush at him if he showed the least sign of wavering. But upon the night of the party his courage vanished, and he thought he would rather face all the dogs in town than knock at the front door.

The parlor was lighted up, and as John stood on the broad flagging before the front door, by the lilac-bush, he could hear the sound of voices—girls' voices—which set his heart in a flutter. He could face the whole district school of girls without flinching,—he didn't mind 'em in the meeting-house in their Sunday best; but he began to be conscious that now he was passing to a new sphere, where the girls are supreme and superior, and he began to feel for the first time that he was an awkward boy. The girl takes to society as naturally as a duckling does to the placid pond, but with a semblance of sly timidity; the boy plunges in with a great splash, and hides his shy awkwardness in noise and commotion.

When John entered, the company had nearly all come. He knew them every one, and yet there was something about them strange and unfamiliar. They were all a little afraid of each other, as people are apt to be when they are well dressed and met together for social purposes in the country. To be at a real party was a novel thing for most of them, and put a constraint upon them which they could not at once overcome. Perhaps it was because they were in the awful parlor, that carpeted room of haircloth furniture, which was so seldom opened. Upon the wall hung two certificates framed in black,—one certifying that, by the payment of fifty dollars, Deacon Mayhew was a life member of the American Tract Society; and the other that, by a like outlay of bread cast upon the waters, his wife was a life member of the A. B. C. F. M., a portion of the alphabet which has an awful significance to all New England childhood. These certificates are a sort of receipt in full for charity, and are a constant and consoling reminder to the farmer that he has discharged his religious duties.

There was a fire on the broad hearth, and that, with the tallow candles on the mantelpiece, made quite an illumination in the room, and enabled the boys, who were mostly on one side of the room, to see the girls, who were on the other, quite plainly. How sweet and demure the girls looked, to be sure! Every boy was thinking if his hair was slick, and feeling the full embarrassment of his entrance into fashionable life. It was queer that these children, who were so free everywhere else, should be so constrained now, and not know what to do with themselves. The shooting of a spark out upon the carpet was a great relief, and was accompanied by a deal of scrambling to throw it back into the fire, and caused much giggling. It was only gradually that the formality was at all broken, and the young people got together and found their tongues.

John at length found himself with Cynthia Rudd, to his great delight and considerable embarrassment, for Cynthia, who was older than John, never looked so pretty. To his surprise he had nothing to say to her. They had always found plenty to talk about before, but now nothing that he could think of seemed worth saying at a party.

"It is a pleasant evening," said John.

"It is quite so," replied Cynthia.

"Did you come in a cutter?" asked John, anxiously.

"No; I walked on the crust, and it was perfectly lovely walking," said Cynthia, in a burst of confidence.

"Was it slippery?" continued John.

"Not very."

John hoped it would be slippery—very—when he walked home with Cynthia, as he determined to do, but he did not dare to say so, and the conversation ran aground again. John thought about his dog and his sled and his yoke of steers, but he didn't see any way to bring them into conversation. Had she read the "Swiss Family Robinson"? Only a little ways. John said it was splendid, and he would lend it to her, for which she thanked him, and said, with such a sweet expression, she should be so glad to have it from him. That was encouraging.

And then John asked Cynthia if she had seen Sally Hawkes since the husking at their house, when Sally found so many red ears; and didn't she think she was a real pretty girl?

"Yes, she was right pretty;" and Cynthia guessed that Sally knew it pretty well. But did John like the color of her eyes?

No; John didn't like the color of her eyes exactly.

"Her mouth would be well enough if she didn't laugh so much and show her teeth."

John said her mouth was her worst feature.

"Oh no," said Cynthia, warmly; "her mouth is better than her nose."

John didn't know but it was better than her nose, and he should like her looks better if her hair wasn't so dreadful black.

But Cynthia, who could afford to be generous now, said she liked black hair, and she wished hers was dark. Whereupon John protested that he liked light hair—auburn hair—of all things.

And Cynthia said that Sally was a dear, good girl, and she didn't believe one word of the story that she only really found one red ear at the husking that night, and hid that and kept pulling it out as if it were a new one.

And so the conversation, once started, went on as briskly as possible about the paring-bee and the spelling-school, and the new singing-master who was coming, and how Jack Thompson had gone to Northampton to be a clerk in a store, and how Elvira Reddington, in the geography class at school, was asked what was the capital of Massachusetts, and had answered "Northampton," and all the school laughed. John enjoyed the conversation amazingly, and he half wished that he and Cynthia were the whole of the party.

But the party had meantime got into operation, and the formality was broken up when the boys and girls had ventured out of the parlor into the more comfortable living-room, with its easy-chairs and everyday things, and even gone so far as to penetrate the kitchen in their frolic. As soon as they forgot they were a party, they began to enjoy themselves.

But the real pleasure only began with the games. The party was nothing without the games, and indeed it was made for the games. Very likely it was one of the timid girls who proposed to play something, and when the ice was once broken, the whole company went into the business enthusiastically. There was no dancing. We should hope not. Not in the deacon's house; not with the deacon's daughters, nor anywhere in this good Puritanic society. Dancing was a sin in itself, and no one could tell what it would lead to. But there was no reason why the boys and girls shouldn't come together and kiss each other during a whole evening occasionally. Kissing was a sign of peace, and was not at all like taking hold of hands and skipping about to the scraping of a wicked fiddle.

In the games there was a great deal of clasping hands, of going round in a circle, of passing under each other's elevated arms, of singing about my true love, and the end was kisses distributed with more or less partiality according to the rules of the play; but, thank Heaven, there was no fiddler. John liked it all, and was quite brave about paying all the forfeits imposed on him, even to the kissing all the girls in the room; but he thought he could have amended that by kissing a few of them a good many times instead of kissing them all once.

But John was destined to have a damper put upon his enjoyment. They were playing a most fascinating game, in which they all stand in a circle and sing a phi-landering song, except one who is in the centre of the ring and holds a cushion. At a certain word in the song, the one in the centre throws the cushion at the feet of some one in the ring, indicating thereby the choice of a mate, and then the two sweetly kneel upon the cushion, like two meek angels, and—and so forth. Then the chosen one takes the cushion and the delightful play goes on. It is very easy, as it will be seen, to learn how to play it. Cynthia was holding the cushion, and at the fatal word she threw it down,—not before John, but in front of Ephraim Leggett. And they two kneeled, and so forth. John was astounded. He had never conceived of such perfidy in the female heart. He felt like wiping Ephraim off the face of the earth, only Ephraim was older and bigger than he. When it came his turn at length—thanks to a plain little girl for whose admiration he didn't care a straw—he threw the cushion down before Melinda Mayhew with all the devotion he could muster, and a dagger look at Cynthia. And Cynthia's perfidious smile only enraged him the more. John felt wronged, and worked himself up to pass a wretched evening.

When supper came he never went near Cynthia, and busied himself in carrying different kinds of pie and cake, and red apples and cider, to the girls he liked the least. He shunned Cynthia, and when he was accidentally near her, and she asked him if he would get her a glass of cider, he rudely told her—like a goose as he was—that she had better ask Ephraim. That seemed to him very smart; but he got more and more miserable, and began to feel that he was making himself ridiculous.

Girls have a great deal more good sense in such matters than boys. Cynthia went to John, at length, and asked him simply what the matter was. John blushed, and said that nothing was the matter. Cynthia said that it wouldn't do for two people always to be together at a party; and so they made up, and John obtained permission to "see" Cynthia home.

**GOING HOME WITH CYNTHIA**

It was after half past nine when the great festivities at the Deacon's broke up, and John walked home with Cynthia over the shining crust and under the stars. It was mostly a silent walk, for this was also an occasion when it is difficult to find anything fit to say. And John was thinking all the way how he should bid Cynthia goodnight; whether it would do and whether it wouldn't do, this not being a game, and no forfeits attaching to it. When they reached the gate there was an awkward little pause. John said the stars were uncommonly bright. Cynthia did not deny it, but waited a minute and then turned abruptly away, with "Good-night, John!"

"Good-night, Cynthia!"

And the party was over, and Cynthia was gone, and John went home in a kind of dissatisfaction with himself.

It was long before he could go to sleep for thinking of the new world opened to him, and imagining how he would act under a hundred different circumstances, and what he would say, and what Cynthia would say; but a dream at length came, and led him away to a great city and a brilliant house; and while he was there he heard a loud rapping on the under floor, and saw that it was daylight.

# XIV

## THE SUGAR CAMP

I THINK there is no part of farming the boy enjoys more than the making of maple sugar; it is better than "blackberrying," and nearly as good as fishing. And one reason he likes this work is that somebody else does the most of it. It is a sort of work in which he can appear to be very active and yet not do much.

And it exactly suits the temperament of a real boy to be very busy about nothing. If the power, for instance, that is expended in play by a boy between the ages of eight and fourteen could be applied to some industry, we should see wonderful results. But a boy is like a galvanic battery that is not in connection with anything: he generates electricity and plays it off into the air with the most reckless prodigality. And I, for one, wouldn't have it otherwise. It is as much a boy's business to play off his energies into space as it is for a flower to blow, or a catbird to sing snatches of the tunes of all the other birds.

In my day, maple-sugar making used to be something between picnicking and being shipwrecked on a fertile island where one should save from the wreck tubs and augers, and great kettles and pork, and hen's-eggs and rye-and-indian bread, and begin at once to lead the sweetest life in the world. I am told that it is something different nowadays, and that there is more desire to save the sap, and make good, pure sugar, and sell it for a large price, than there used to be, and that the old fun and picturesqueness of the business are pretty much gone. I am told that it is the custom to carefully collect the sap and bring it to the house, where there are built brick arches, over which it is evaporated in shallow pans; and that pains is taken to keep the leaves, sticks, and ashes and coals out of it; and that the sugar is clarified; and that, in short, it is a money-making business, in which there is very little fun, and that the boy is not allowed to dip his paddle into the kettle of boiling sugar and lick off the delicious sirup. The prohibition may improve the sugar, but it is cruel to the boy.

As I remember the New England boy (and I am very intimate with one), he used to be on the *qui vive* in the spring for the sap to begin running. I think he discovered it as soon as anybody. Perhaps he knew it by a feeling of something starting in his own veins,—a sort of spring stir in his legs and arms, which tempted him to stand on his head, or throw a handspring, if he could find a spot of ground from which the snow had melted. The sap stirs early in the legs of a country boy, and shows itself in uneasiness in the toes, which get tired of boots, and want to come out and touch the soil just as soon as the sun has warmed it a little. The country boy goes barefoot just as naturally as the trees burst their buds, which were packed and varnished over in the fall to keep the water and the frost out. Perhaps the boy has been out digging into the maple-trees with his jack-knife; at any rate, he is pretty sure to announce the discovery as he comes running into the house in a great state of excitement—as if he had heard a hen cackle in the barn—with, "Sap's runnin'!"

And then, indeed, the stir and excitement begin. The sap-buckets, which have been stored in the garret over the woodhouse, and which the boy has occasionally climbed up to look at with another boy, for they are full of sweet suggestions of the annual spring frolic,—the sap-buckets are brought down and set out on the south side of the house and scalded. The snow is still a foot or two feet deep in the woods, and the ox-sled is got out to make a road to the sugar camp, and the campaign begins. The boy is everywhere present, superintending everything, asking questions, and filled with a desire to help the excitement.

It is a great day when the cart is loaded with the buckets and the procession starts into the woods. The sun shines almost unobstructedly into the forest, for there are only naked branches to bar it; the snow is soft and beginning to sink down, leaving the young bushes spindling up everywhere; the snow-birds are twittering about, and the noise of shouting and of the blows of the axe echoes far and wide. This is spring, and the boy can scarcely contain his delight that his outdoor life is about to begin again.

In the first place the men go about and tap the trees, drive in the spouts, and hang the buckets under. The boy watches all these operations with the greatest interest. He wishes that some time when a hole is bored in a tree that the sap would spout out in a stream as it does when a cider-barrel is tapped; but it never does, it only drops, sometimes almost in a stream, but on the whole slowly, and the boy learns that the sweet things of the world have to be patiently waited for, and do not usually come otherwise than drop by drop.

Then the camp is to be cleared of snow. The shanty is re-covered with boughs. In front of it two enormous logs are rolled nearly together, and a fire is built between them. Forked sticks are set at each end, and a long pole is laid on them, and on this are hung the great caldron kettles. The huge hogsheads are turned right side up, and cleaned out to receive the sap that is gathered. And now, if there is a good "sap run," the establishment is under full headway.

The great fire that is kindled up is never let out, night or day, as long as the season lasts. Somebody is always cutting wood to feed it; somebody is busy most of the time gathering in the sap; somebody is required to watch the kettles that they do not boil over, and to fill them. It is not the boy, however; he is too busy with things in general to be of any use in details. He has his own little sap-yoke and small pails, with which he gathers the sweet liquid. He has a little boiling-place of his own, with small logs and a tiny kettle. In the great kettles the boiling goes on slowly, and the liquid, as it thickens, is dipped from one to another, until in the end kettle it is reduced to sirup, and is taken out to cool and settle, until enough is made to "sugar off." To "sugar off" is to boil the sirup until it is thick enough to crystallize into sugar. This is the grand event, and it is only done once in two or three days.

**A YOUNG SUGAR-MAKER**

But the boy's desire is to "sugar off" perpetually. He boils his kettle down as rapidly as possible; he is not particular about chips, scum, or ashes; he is apt to burn his sugar; but if he can get enough to make a little wax on the snow, or to scrape from the bottom of the kettle with his wooden paddle, he is happy. A good deal is wasted on his hands and the outside of his face and on his clothes, but he does not care; he is not stingy.

To watch the operations of the big fire gives him constant pleasure. Sometimes he is left to watch the boiling kettles, with a piece of pork tied on the end of a stick, which he dips into the boiling mass when it threatens to go over. He is constantly tasting of it, however, to see if it is not almost sirup. He has a long round stick, whittled smooth at one end, which he uses for this purpose, at the constant risk of burning his tongue. The smoke blows in his face; he is grimy with ashes; he is altogether such a mass of dirt, stickiness, and sweetness, that his own mother wouldn't know him.

He likes to boil eggs with the hired man in the hot sap; he likes to roast potatoes in the ashes, and he would live in the camp day and night if he were permitted. Some of the hired men sleep in the bough shanty and keep the fire blazing all night. To sleep there with them, and awake in the night and hear the wind in the trees, and see the sparks fly up to the sky, is a perfect realization of all the stories of adventures he has ever read. He tells the other boys afterwards that he heard something in the night that sounded very much like a bear. The hired man says that he was very much scared by the hooting of an owl.

The great occasions for the boy, though, are the times of "sugaring off." Sometimes this used to be done in the evening, and it was made the excuse for a frolic in the camp. The neighbors were invited; sometimes even the pretty girls from the village, who filled all the woods with their sweet voices and merry laughter and little affectations of fright. The white snow still lies on all the ground except the warm spot about the camp. The tree branches all show distinctly in the light of the fire, which sends its ruddy glare far into the darkness, and lights up the bough shanty, the hogsheads, the buckets on the trees, and the group about the boiling kettles, until the scene is like something taken out of a fairy play. If Rembrandt could have seen a sugar party in a New England wood, he would have made out of its strong contrasts of light and shade one of the finest pictures in the world. But Rembrandt was not born in Massachusetts; people hardly ever do know where to be born until it is too late. Being born in the right place is a thing that has been very much neglected.

At these sugar parties every one was expected to eat as much sugar as possible; and those who are practiced in it can eat a great deal. It is a peculiarity about eating warm maple-sugar that, though you may eat so much of it one day as to be sick and loathe the thought of it, you will want it the next day more than ever. At the "sugaring off" they used to pour the hot sugar upon the snow, where it congealed, without crystallizing, into a sort of wax, which I do suppose is the most delicious substance that was ever invented. And it takes a great while to eat it. If one should close his teeth firmly on a ball of it, he would be unable to open his mouth until it dissolved. The sensation while it is melting is very pleasant, but one cannot converse.

## WATCHING THE KETTLES

The boy used to make a big lump of it and give it to the dog, who seized it with great avidity, and closed his jaws on it, as dogs will on anything. It was funny the next moment to see the expression of perfect surprise on the dog's face when he found that he could not open his jaws. He shook his head; he sat down in despair; he ran round in a circle; he dashed into the woods and back again. He did everything except climb a tree and howl. It would have been such a relief to him if he could have howled! But that was the one thing he could not do.

# XV

## THE HEART OF NEW ENGLAND

Iᴛ is a wonder that every New England boy does not turn out a poet, or a
missionary, or a peddler. Most of them used to. There is everything in the heart of
the New England hills to feed the imagination of the boy, and excite his longing
for strange countries. I scarcely know what the subtle influence is that forms him
and attracts him in the most fascinating and aromatic of all lands, and yet urges
him away from all the sweet delights of his home to become a roamer in literature
and in the world,—a poet and a wanderer. There is something in the soil and the
pure air, I suspect, that promises more romance than is forthcoming, that excites
the imagination without satisfying it, and begets the desire of adventure. And the
prosaic life of the sweet home does not at all correspond to the boy's dreams of the
world. In the good old days, I am told, the boys on the coast ran away and became
sailors; the country boys waited till they grew big enough to be missionaries, and
then they sailed away, and met the coast boys in foreign ports.

John used to spend hours in the top of a slender hickory-tree that a little detached itself from the forest which crowned the brow of the steep and lofty pasture behind his house. He was sent to make war on the bushes that constantly
encroached upon the pasture land; but John had no hostility to any growing thing,
and a very little bushwhacking satisfied him. When he had grubbed up a few lau-
rels and young treesprouts, he was wont to retire into his favorite post of observation and meditation. Perhaps he fancied that the wide-swaying stem to which he
clung was the mast of a ship; that the tossing forest behind him was the heaving
waves of the sea; and that the wind which moaned over the woods and murmured
in the leaves, and now and then sent him a wide circuit in the air, as if he had been
a blackbird on the tiptop of a spruce, was an ocean gale. What life and action and
heroism there was to him in the multitudinous roar of the forest, and what an eter-
nity of existence in the monologue of the river which brawled far, far below him
over its wide stony bed! How the river sparkled and danced and went on—now
in a smooth amber current, now fretted by the pebbles, but always with that continuous busy song! John never knew that noise to cease, and he doubted not if he
stayed here a thousand years that same loud murmur would fill the air.

On it went, under the wide spans of the old wooden, covered bridge, swirling
around the great rocks on which the piers stood, spreading away below in shal-
lows, and taking the shadows of a row of maples that lined the green shore. Save
this roar, no sound reached him, except now and then the rumble of a wagon on
the bridge, or the muffled, far-off voices of some chance passers on the road. Seen

from this high perch, the familiar village, sending its brown roofs and white spires up through the green foliage, had a strange aspect, and was like some town in a book, say a village nestled in the Swiss mountains, or something in Bohemia. And there, beyond the purple hills of Bozrah, and not so far as the stony pastures of Zoar, whither John had helped drive the colts and young stock in the spring, might be perhaps Jerusalem itself. John had himself once been to the land of Canaan with his grandfather, when he was a very small boy; and he had once seen an actual, no-mistake Jew, a mysterious person, with uncut beard and long hair, who sold scythe-snaths in that region, and about whom there was a rumor that he was once caught and shaved by the indignant farmers, who apprehended in his long locks a contempt of the Christian religion. Oh, the world had vast possibilities for John. Away to the south, up a vast basin of forest, there was a notch in the horizon and an opening in the line of woods, where the road ran. Through this opening John imagined an army might appear, perhaps British, perhaps Turks, and banners of red and of yellow advance, and a cannon wheel about and point its long nose and open on the valley. He fancied the army, after this salute, winding down the mountain road, deploying in the meadows, and giving the valley to pillage and to flame. In which event his position would be an excellent one for observation and for safety. While he was in the height of this engagement, perhaps the horn would be blown from the back porch, reminding him that it was time to quit cutting brush and go for the cows. As if there were no better use for a warrior and a poet in New England than to send him for the cows!

**THE VILLAGE FROM THE HILL**

John knew a boy—a bad enough boy, I dare say—who afterwards became a general in the war, and went to Congress and got to be a real governor, who used also to be sent to cut brush in the back pastures, and hated it in his very soul; and by his wrong conduct forecast what kind of a man he would be. This boy, as soon as he had cut about one brush, would seek for one of several holes in the ground (and he was familiar with several), in which lived a white-and-black animal that must always be nameless in a book, but an animal quite capable of the most pungent defense of himself. This young aspirant to Congress would cut a long stick, with a little crotch in the end of it, and run it into the hole; and when the crotch was punched into the fur and skin of the animal, he would twist the stick round till it got a good grip on the skin, and then he would pull the beast out; and when he got the white-and-black just out of the hole so that his dog could seize him, the boy would take to his heels, and leave the two to fight it out, content to scent the battle afar off. And this boy, who was in training for public life, would do this sort of thing all the afternoon; and when the sun told him that he had spent long enough time cutting brush, he would industriously go home as innocent as anybody. There are few such boys as this nowadays; and that is the reason why the New England pastures are so much overgrown with brush.

John himself preferred to hunt the pugnacious woodchuck. He bore a special grudge against this clover-eater, beyond the usual hostility that boys feel for any wild animal. One day on his way to school a woodchuck crossed the road before him, and John gave chase. The woodchuck scrambled into an orchard and climbed a small apple-tree. John thought this a most cowardly and unfair retreat, and stood under the tree and taunted the animal and stoned it. Thereupon the woodchuck dropped down on John and seized him by the leg of his trousers. John was both enraged and scared by this dastardly attack; the teeth of the enemy went through the cloth and met; and there he hung. John then made a pivot of one leg and whirled himself around, swinging the woodchuck in the air, until he shook him off; but in his departure the woodchuck carried away a large piece of John's summer trousers leg. The boy never forgot it. And whenever he had a holiday he used to expend an amount of labor and ingenuity in the pursuit of woodchucks that would have made his fortune in any useful pursuit. There was a hill-pasture, down on one side of which ran a small brook, and this pasture was full of woodchuck-holes. It required the assistance of several boys to capture a woodchuck. It was first necessary by patient watching to ascertain that the woodchuck was at home. When one was seen to enter his burrow, then all the entries to it except one—there are usually three—were plugged up with stones. A boy and a dog were then left to watch the open hole, while John and his comrades went to the brook and began to dig a canal, to turn the water into the residence of the woodchuck. This was often a difficult feat of engineering and a long job. Often it took more than half a day of hard labor with shovel and hoe to dig the canal. But when the canal was finished, and the water began to pour into the hole, the excitement began. How long would it take to fill the hole and drown out the woodchuck? Sometimes it seemed as if the hole were a bottomless pit. But sooner or later the water would rise in it, and then there was sure to be seen the nose of the woodchuck, keeping itself on a level with the rising flood. It was piteous to see the anxious look of the hunted, half-drowned creature as it came to the surface and caught sight of the dog. There the dog stood, at the mouth of the hole, quivering with excitement from his nose to the tip of his tail, and behind him were the cruel boys dancing with joy and setting the dog on. The poor creature would disappear in the water in terror; but he must breathe, and out would come his nose again, nearer the dog each time. At last the water ran out of the hole as well as in, and the soaked beast came with it, and made a desperate rush. But in a trice the dog had him, and the boys stood off in a circle, with stones in their hands, to see what they called "fair play." They maintained perfect "neutrality" so long as the dog was getting the best of the woodchuck; but if the latter was likely to escape, they "interfered" in the interest of peace and the "balance of power," and killed the woodchuck. This is a boy's notion of justice; of course he'd no business to be a woodchuck,—an "unspeakable woodchuck."

**TREEING A WOODCHUCK**

I used the word "aromatic" in relation to the New England soil. John knew very well all its sweet, aromatic, pungent, and medicinal products, and liked to search for the scented herbs and the wild fruits and exquisite flowers; but he did not then know, and few do know, that there is no part of the globe where the subtle chemistry of the earth produces more that is agreeable to the senses than a New England hill-pasture and the green meadow at its foot. The poets have succeeded in turning our attention from it to the comparatively barren Orient as the land of sweet-smelling spices and odorous gums. And it is indeed a constant surprise that this poor and stony soil elaborates and grows so many delicate and aromatic products.

John, it is true, did not care much for anything that did not appeal to his taste and smell and delight in brilliant color; and he trod down the exquisite ferns and the wonderful mosses without compunction. But he gathered from the crevices of the rocks the columbine and the eglantine and the blue harebell; he picked the high-flavored alpine strawberry, the blueberry, the boxberry, wild currants and gooseberries and fox-grapes; he brought home armfuls of the pink-and-white laurel and the wild honeysuckle; he dug the roots of the fragrant sassafras and of the sweet-flag; he ate the tender leaves of the wintergreen and its red berries; he gathered the peppermint and the spearmint; he gnawed the twigs of the black birch; there was a stout fern which he called "brake," which he pulled up, and found that the soft end "tasted good;" he dug the amber gum from the spruce-tree, and liked to smell, though he could not chew, the gum of the wild cherry; it was his melancholy duty to bring home such medicinal herbs for the garret as the gold-thread, the tansy, and the loathsome "boneset;" and he laid in for the winter, like a squirrel, stores of beech-nuts, hazel-nuts, hickory-nuts, chestnuts, and butternuts. But that which lives most vividly in his memory and most strongly draws him back to the New England hills is the aromatic sweet-fern: he likes to eat its spicy seeds, and to crush in his hands its fragrant leaves; their odor is the unique essence of New England.

# XVI

## JOHN'S REVIVAL

THE New England country boy of the last generation never heard of Christmas.

There was no such day in his calendar. If John ever came across it in his reading, he attached no meaning to the word.

If his curiosity had been aroused, and he had asked his elders about it, he might have got the dim impression that it was a kind of Popish holiday, the celebration of which was about as wicked as "card-playing," or being a "democrat." John knew a couple of desperately bad boys who were reported to play "seven-up" in a barn, on the hay-mow, and the enormity of this practice made him shudder. He had once seen a pack of greasy "playing-cards," and it seemed to him to contain the quintessence of sin. If he had desired to defy all Divine law and outrage all human society, he felt that he could do it by shuffling them. And he was quite right. The two bad boys enjoyed in stealth their scandalous pastime, because they knew it was the most wicked thing they could do. If it had been as sinless as playing marbles, they wouldn't have cared for it. John sometimes drove past a brown, tumble-down farm-house, whose shiftless inhabitants, it was said, were card-playing people; and it is impossible to describe how wicked that house appeared to John. He almost expected to see its shingles stand on end. In the old New England, one could not in any other way so express his contempt of all holy and orderly life as by playing cards for amusement.

There was no element of Christmas in John's life, any more than there was of Easter, and probably nobody about him could have explained Easter; and he escaped all the demoralization attending Christmas gifts. Indeed, he never had any presents of any kind, either on his birthday or any other day. He expected nothing that he did not earn, or make in the way of "trade" with another boy. He was taught to work for what he received. He even earned, as I said, the extra holidays of the day after the "Fourth" and the day after Thanksgiving. Of the free grace and gifts of Christmas he had no conception. The single and melancholy association he had with it was the quaking hymn which his grandfather used to sing in a cracked and quavering voice, —

> "While shepherds watched their flocks by night,
> All seated on the ground."

The "glory" that "shone around" at the end of it—the doleful voice always repeating, "and glory shone around"—made John as miserable as "Hark! from the tombs." It was all one dreary expectation of something uncomfortable. It was, in short, "religion." You'd got to have it some time; that John believed. But it lay in his unthinking mind to put off the "Hark! from the tombs" enjoyment as long as possible. He experienced a kind of delightful wickedness in indulging his dislike of hymns and of Sunday.

**LOOKING FOR FROGS**

John was not a model boy, but I cannot exactly define in what his wickedness consisted. He had no inclination to steal, nor much to lie; and he despised "meanness" and stinginess, and had a chivalrous feeling toward little girls. Probably it never occurred to him that there was any virtue in not stealing and lying, for honesty and veracity were in the atmosphere about him. He hated work, and he "got mad" easily; but he did work, and he was always ashamed when he was over his fit of passion. In short, you couldn't find a much better wicked boy than John.

When the "revival" came, therefore, one summer, John was in a quandary. Sunday meeting and Sunday school he didn't mind; they were a part of regular life, and only temporarily interrupted a boy's pleasures. But when there began to be evening meetings at the different houses, a new element came into affairs. There was a kind of solemnity over the community, and a seriousness in all faces. At first these twilight assemblies offered a little relief to the monotony of farm-life; and John liked to meet the boys and girls, and to watch the older people coming in, dressed in their second best. I think John's imagination was worked upon by the sweet and mournful hymns that were discordantly sung in the stiff old parlors. There was a suggestion of Sunday, and sanctity too, in the odor of caraway-seed that pervaded the room. The windows were wide open also, and the scent of June roses came in with all the languishing sounds of a summer night. All the little boys had a scared look, but the little girls were never so pretty and demure as in this their susceptible seriousness. If John saw a boy who did not come to the evening meeting, but was wandering off with his sling down the meadow, looking for frogs, maybe, that boy seemed to him a monster of wickedness.

After a time, as the meetings continued, John fell also under the general impression of fright and seriousness. All the talk was of "getting religion," and he heard over and over again that the probability was, if he did not get it now he never would. The chance did not come often, and, if this offer was not improved, John would be given over to hardness of heart. His obstinacy would show that he was not one of the elect. John fancied that he could feel his heart hardening, and he began to look with a wistful anxiety into the faces of the Christians to see what were the visible signs of being one of the elect. John put on a good deal of a manner that he "didn't care," and he never admitted his disquiet by asking any questions or standing up in meeting to be prayed for. But he did care. He heard all the time that all he had to do was to repent and believe. But there was nothing that he doubted, and he was perfectly willing to repent if he could think of anything to repent of.

It was essential, he learned, that he should have a "conviction of sin." This he earnestly tried to have. Other people, no better than he, had it, and he wondered why he couldn't have it. Boys and girls whom he knew were "under conviction," and John began to feel not only panicky but lonesome. Cynthia Rudd had been anxious for days and days, and not able to sleep at night, but now she had given herself up and found peace. There was a kind of radiance in her face that struck John with awe, and he felt that now there was a great gulf between him and Cynthia. Everybody was going away from him, and his heart was getting harder than ever. He couldn't feel wicked, all he could do. And there was Ed Bates, his intimate friend, though older than he, a "whaling," noisy kind of boy, who was under conviction and sure he was going to be lost. How John envied him! And, pretty soon, Ed "experienced religion." John anxiously watched the change in Ed's face when he became one of the elect. And a change there was. And John wondered about another thing. Ed Bates used to go trout-fishing, with a tremendously long pole, in a meadow-brook near the river; and when the trout didn't bite right off Ed would "get mad," and as soon as one took hold he would give an awful jerk, sending the fish more than three hundred feet into the air and landing it in the bushes the other side of the meadow, crying out, "Gul darn ye, I'll learn ye." And John wondered if Ed would take the little trout out any more gently now.

## TROUT FISHING

John felt more and more lonesome as one after another of his playmates came out and made a profession. Cynthia (she too was older than John) sat on Sunday in the singers' seat; her voice, which was going to be a contralto, had a wonderful pathos in it for him, and he heard it with a heartache. "There she is," thought John, "singing away like an angel in heaven, and I am left out." During all his after life a contralto voice was to John one of his most bitter and heart-wringing pleasures. It suggested the immaculate scornful, the melancholy unattainable.

If ever a boy honestly tried to work himself into a conviction of sin, John tried. And what made him miserable was that he couldn't feel miserable when everybody else was miserable. He even began to pretend to be so. He put on a serious and anxious look like the others. He pretended he didn't care for play; he refrained from chasing chipmunks and snaring suckers; the songs of birds and the bright vivacity of the summer time that used to make him turn hand-springs smote him as a discordant levity. He was not a hypocrite at all, and he was getting to be alarmed that he was not alarmed at himself. Every day and night he heard that the spirit of the Lord would probably soon quit striving with him, and leave him out. The phrase was that he would "grieve away the Holy Spirit." John wondered if he was not doing it. He did everything to put himself in the way of conviction, was constant at the evening meetings, wore a grave face, refrained from play, and tried to feel anxious. At length he concluded that he must do something.

One night as he walked home from a solemn meeting, at which several of his little playmates had "come forward," he felt that he could force the crisis. He was alone on the sandy road: it was an enchanting summer night; the stars danced overhead, and by his side the broad and shallow river ran over its stony bed with a loud but soothing murmur that filled all the air with entreaty, John did not then know that it sang, "But I go on forever," yet there was in it for him something of the solemn flow of the eternal world. When he came in sight of the house, he knelt down in the dust by a pile of rails and prayed. He prayed that he might feel bad, and be distressed about himself. As he prayed he heard distinctly, and yet not as a disturbance, the multitudinous croaking of the frogs by the meadow-spring. It was not discordant with his thoughts; it had in it a melancholy pathos, as if it were a kind of call to the unconverted. What is there in this sound that suggests the tenderness of spring, the despair of a summer night, the desolateness of young love? Years after it happened to John to be at twilight at a railway station on the edge of the Ravenna marshes. A little way over the purple plain he saw the darkening towers and heard "the sweet bells of Imola." The Holy Pontiff Pius IX. was born at Imola, and passed his boyhood in that serene and moist region. As the train waited, John heard from miles of marshes round about the evening song of millions of frogs, louder and more melancholy and entreating than the vesper call of the bells. And instantly his mind went back—for the association of sound is as subtle as that of odor—to the prayer, years ago, by the roadside and the plaintive appeal of the unheeded frogs, and he wondered if the little Pope had not heard the like importunity, and perhaps, when he thought of himself as a little Pope, associated his conversion with this plaintive sound.

John prayed, but without feeling any worse, and then went desperately into the house and told the family that he was in an anxious state of mind. This was joyful news to the sweet and pious household, and the little boy was urged to feel that he was a sinner, to repent, and to become that night a Christian; he was prayed over, and told to read the Bible, and put to bed with the injunction to repeat all the texts of Scripture and hymns he could think of. John did this, and said over and over the few texts he was master of, and tossed about in a real discontent now, for he had a dim notion that he was playing the hypocrite a little. But he was sincere enough in wanting to feel, as the other boys and girls felt, that he was a wicked sinner. He tried to think of his evil deeds; and one occurred to him, indeed, it often came to his mind. It was a lie,—a deliberate, awful lie, that never injured anybody but himself. John knew he was not wicked enough to tell a lie to injure anybody else.

This was the lie. One afternoon at school, just before John's class was to recite in geography, his pretty cousin, a young lady he held in great love and respect, came in to visit the school. John was a favorite with her, and she had come to hear him recite. As it happened, John felt shaky in the geographical lesson of that day, and he feared to be humiliated in the presence of his cousin; he felt embarrassed to that degree that he couldn't have "bounded" Massachusetts. So he stood up and raised his hand, and said to the schoolma'am, "Please, ma'am, I've got the stomach-ache; may I go home?" And John's character for truthfulness was so high (and even this was ever a reproach to him) that his word was instantly believed, and he was dismissed without any medical examination. For a moment John was delighted to get out of school so early; but soon his guilt took all the light out of the summer sky and the pleasantness out of nature. He had to walk slowly, without a single hop or jump, as became a diseased boy. The sight of a woodchuck at a distance from his well-known hole tempted John, but he restrained himself, lest somebody should see him, and know that chasing a woodchuck was inconsistent with the stomach-ache. He was acting a miserable part, but it had to be gone through with. He went home and told his mother the reason he had left school, but he added that he felt "some" better now. The "some" didn't save him. Genuine sympathy was lavished on him. He had to swallow a stiff dose of nasty "picra," the horror of all childhood, and he was put in bed immediately. The world never looked so pleasant to John, but to bed he was forced to go. He was excused from all chores; he was not even to go after the cows. John said he thought he ought to go after the cows,—much as he hated the business usually, he would now willingly have wandered over the world after cows,—and for this heroic offer, in the condition he was, he got credit for a desire to do his duty; and this unjust confidence in him added to his torture. And he had intended to set his hooks that night for eels. His cousin came home, and sat by his bedside and condoled with him; his schoolma'am had sent word how sorry she was for him, John was such a good boy. All this was dreadful. He groaned in agony. Besides, he was not to have any supper; it would be very dangerous to eat a morsel. The prospect was appalling. Never was there such a long twilight; never before did he hear so many sounds outdoors that he wanted to investigate. Being ill without any illness was a horrible condition. And he began to have real stomach-ache now; and it ached because it was empty. John was hungry enough to have eaten the New England Primer. But by and by sleep came, and John forgot his woes in dreaming that he knew where Madagascar was just as easy as anything.

It was this lie that came back to John the night he was trying to be affected by the revival. And he was very much ashamed of it, and believed he would never tell another. But then he fell thinking whether with the "picra," and the going to bed in the afternoon, and the loss of his supper, he had not been sufficiently paid for it. And in this unhopeful frame of mind he dropped off in sleep.

And the truth must be told, that in the morning John was no nearer to realizing the terrors he desired to feel. But he was a conscientious boy, and would do nothing to interfere with the influences of the season. He not only put himself away from them all, but he refrained from doing almost everything that he wanted to do. There came at that time a newspaper, a secular newspaper, which had in it a long account of the Long Island races, in which the famous horse "Lexington" was a runner. John was fond of horses, he knew about Lexington, and he had looked forward to the result of this race with keen interest. But to read the account of it now he felt might destroy his seriousness of mind, and—in all reverence and simplicity he felt it—be a means of "grieving away the Holy Spirit." He therefore hid away the paper in a table drawer, intending to read it when the revival should be over. Weeks after, when he looked for the newspaper, it was not to be found, and John never knew what "time" Lexington made, nor anything about the race. This was to him a serious loss, but by no means so deep as another feeling that remained with him; for when his little world returned to its ordinary course, and long after, John had an uneasy apprehension of his own separateness from other people in his insensibility to the revival. Perhaps the experience was a damage to him; and it is a pity that there was no one to explain that religion for a little fellow like him is not a "scheme."

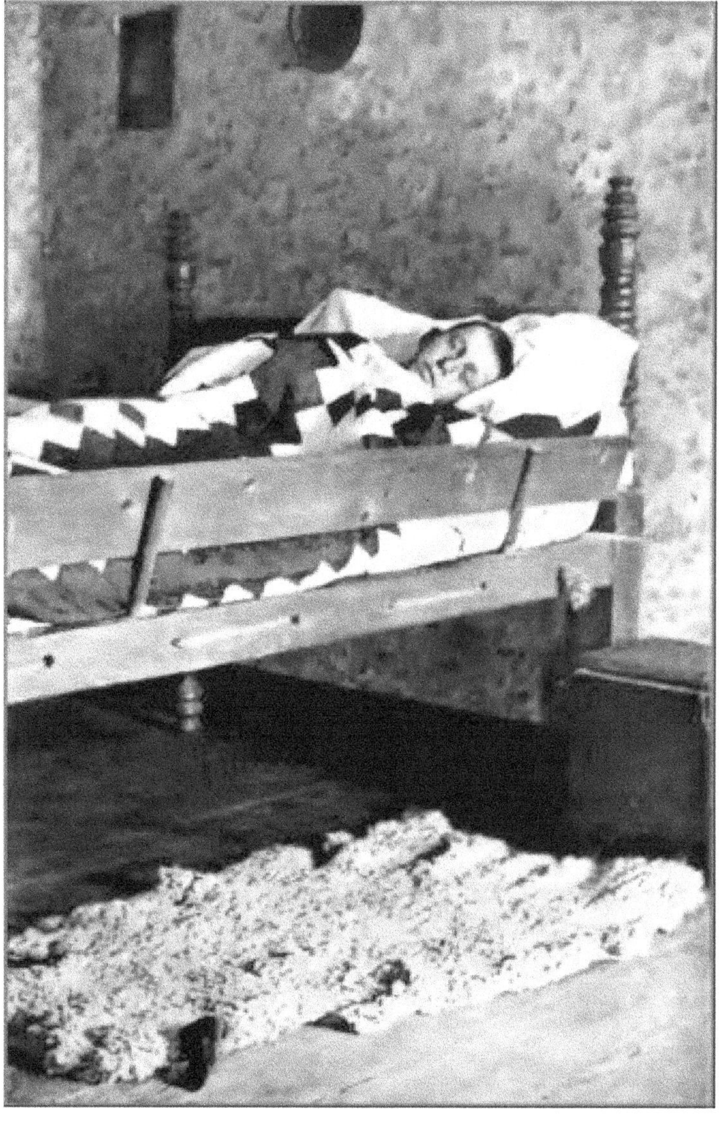

**FORCED TO GO TO BED**

# XVII

## WAR

Every boy who is good for anything is a natural savage. The scientists who want to study the primitive man, and have so much difficulty in finding one anywhere in this sophisticated age, couldn't do better than to devote their attention to the common country boy. He has the primal, vigorous instincts and impulses of the African savage, without any of the vices inherited from a civilization long ago decayed, or developed in an unrestrained barbaric society. You want to catch your boy young, and study him before he has either virtues or vices, in order to understand the primitive man.

Every New England boy desires (or did desire a generation ago, before children were born sophisticated, with a large library, and with the word "culture" written on their brows) to live by hunting, fishing, and war. The military instinct, which is the special mark of barbarism, is strong in him. It arises not alone from his love of fighting, for the boy is naturally as cowardly as the savage, but from his fondness for display,—the same that a corporal or a general feels in decking himself in tinsel and tawdry colors and strutting about in view of the female sex. Half the pleasure in going out to murder another man with a gun would be wanting if one did not wear feathers and gold lace and stripes on his pantaloons. The law also takes this view of it, and will not permit men to shoot each other in plain clothes. And the world also makes some curious distinctions in the art of killing. To kill people with arrows is barbarous; to kill them with smooth-bores and flint-lock muskets is semi-civilized; to kill them with breech-loading rifles is civilized. That nation is the most civilized which has the appliances to kill the most of another nation in the shortest time. This is the result of six thousand years of constant civilization. By and by, when the nations cease to be boys, perhaps they will not want to kill each other at all. Some people think the world is very old; but here is an evidence that it is very young, and, in fact, has scarcely yet begun to be a world. When the volcanoes have done spouting, and the earthquakes are quaked out, and you can tell what land is going to be solid and keep its level twenty-four hours, and the swamps are filled up, and the deltas of the great rivers, like the Mississippi and the Nile, become *terra firma*, and men stop killing their fellows in order to get their land and other property, then perhaps there will be a world that an angel wouldn't weep over. Now one half the world are employed in getting ready to kill the other half, some of them by marching about in uniform, and the others by hard work to earn money to pay taxes to buy uniforms and guns.

John was not naturally very cruel, and it was probably the love of display quite as much as of fighting that led him into a military life; for he in common with all his comrades had other traits of the savage. One of them was the same passion for ornament that induces the African to wear anklets and bracelets of hide and of metal, and to decorate himself with tufts of hair, and to tattoo his body. In John's day there was a rage at school among the boys for wearing bracelets woven of the hair of the little girls. Some of them were wonderful specimens of braiding and twist. These were not captured in war, but were sentimental tokens of friendship given by the young maidens themselves. John's own hair was kept so short (as became a warrior) that you couldn't have made a bracelet out of it, or anything except a paint-brush; but the little girls were not under military law, and they willingly sacrificed their tresses to decorate the soldiers they esteemed. As the Indian is honored in proportion to the scalps he can display, the boy at John's school was held in highest respect who could show the most hair trophies on his wrist. John himself had a variety that would have pleased a Mohawk, fine and coarse and of all colors. There were the flaxen, the faded straw, the glossy black, the lustrous brown, the dirty yellow, the undecided auburn, and the fiery red. Perhaps his pulse beat more quickly under the red hair of Cynthia Rudd than on account of all the other wristlets put together; it was a sort of gold-tried-in-the-fire color to John, and burned there with a steady flame. Now that Cynthia had become a Christian, this band of hair seemed a more sacred if less glowing possession (for all detached hair will fade in time), and if he had known anything about saints he would have imagined that it was a part of the aureole that always goes with a saint. But I am bound to say that, while John had a tender feeling for this red string, his sentiment was not that of the man who becomes entangled in the meshes of a woman's hair; and he valued rather the number than the quality of these elastic wristlets.

John burned with as real a military ardor as ever inflamed the breast of any slaughterer of his fellows. He liked to read of war, of encounters with the Indians, of any kind of wholesale killing in glittering uniform, to the noise of the terribly exciting fife and drum, which maddened the combatants and drowned the cries of the wounded. In his future he saw himself a soldier with plume and sword and snug-fitting, decorated clothes,—very different from his somewhat roomy trousers and country-cut roundabout, made by Aunt Ellis, the village tailoress, who cut out clothes, not according to the shape of the boy, but to what he was expected to grow to,—going where glory awaited him. In his observation of pictures, it was the common soldier who was always falling and dying, while the officer stood unharmed in the storm of bullets and waved his sword in a heroic attitude. John determined to be an officer.

It is needless to say that he was an ardent member of the military company of his village. He had risen from the grade of corporal to that of first lieutenant; the captain was a boy whose father was captain of the grown militia company, and consequently had inherited military aptness and knowledge. The old captain was a flaming son of Mars, whose nose militia war, general training, and New England rum had painted with the color of glory and disaster. He was one of the gallant old soldiers of the peaceful days of our country, splendid in uniform, a martinet in drill, terrible in oaths, a glorious object when he marched at the head of his company of flintlock muskets, with the American banner full high advanced, and the clamorous drum defying the world. In this he fulfilled his duties of citizen, faithfully teaching his uniformed companions how to march by the left leg, and to get reeling drunk by sundown; otherwise he didn't amount to much in the community; his house was unpainted, his fences were tumbled down, his farm was a waste, his wife wore an old gown to meeting, to which the captain never went; but he was a good trout-fisher, and there was no man in town who spent more time at the country store and made more shrewd observations upon the affairs of his neighbors. Although he had never been in an asylum any more than he had been in war, he was almost as perfect a drunkard as he was soldier. He hated the British, whom he had never seen, as much as he loved rum, from which he was never separated.

The company which his son commanded, wearing his father's belt and sword, was about as effective as the old company, and more orderly. It contained from thirty to fifty boys, according to the pressure of "chores" at home, and it had its great days of parade and its autumn manoeuvres, like the general training. It was an artillery company, which gave every boy a chance to wear a sword; and it possessed a small mounted cannon, which was dragged about and limbered and unlimbered and fired, to the imminent danger of everybody, especially of the company. In point of marching, with all the legs going together, and twisting itself up and untwisting, breaking into single-file (for Indian fighting) and forming platoons, turning a sharp corner, and getting out of the way of a wagon, circling the town pump, frightening horses, stopping short in front of the tavern, with ranks dressed and eyes right and left, it was the equal of any military organization I ever saw. It could train better than the big company, and I think it did more good in keeping alive the spirit of patriotism and desire to fight. Its discipline was strict. If a boy left the ranks to jab a spectator, or make faces at a window, or "go for" a striped snake, he was "hollered" at no end.

It was altogether a very serious business; there was no levity about the hot and hard marching, and as boys have no humor nothing ludicrous occurred. John was very proud of his office, and of his ability to keep the rear ranks closed up and ready to execute any manoeuvre when the captain "hollered," which he did continually. He carried a real sword, which his grandfather had worn in many a militia campaign on the village green, the rust upon which John fancied was Indian blood; he had various red and yellow insignia of military rank sewed upon different parts of his clothes, and though his cocked hat was of pasteboard, it was decorated with gilding and bright rosettes, and floated a red feather that made his heart beat with martial fury whenever he looked at it. The effect of this uniform upon the girls was not a matter of conjecture. I think they really cared nothing about it, but they pretended to think it fine, and they fed the poor boys' vanity,—the weakness by which women govern the world.

The exalted happiness of John in this military service I dare say was never equalled in any subsequent occupation. The display of the company in the village filled him with the loftiest heroism. There was nothing wanting but an enemy to fight, but this could only be had by half the company staining themselves with elderberry juice and going into the woods as Indians, to fight the artillery from behind trees with bows and arrows, or to ambush it and tomahawk the gunners. This, however, was made to seem very like real war. Traditions of Indian cruelty were still fresh in Western Massachusetts. Behind John's house in the orchard were some old slate tombstones, sunken and leaning, which recorded the names of Captain Moses Rice and Phineas Arms, who had been killed by Indians in the last century while at work in the meadow by the river, and who slept there in the hope of a glorious resurrection. Phineas Arms—martial name—was long since dust; and even the mortal part of the great Captain Moses Rice had been absorbed in the soil, and passed perhaps with the sap up into the old but still blooming apple-trees. It was a quiet place where they lay, but they might have heard—if hear they could—the loud, continuous roar of the Deerfield, and the stirring of the long grass on that sunny slope. There was a tradition that years ago an Indian, probably the last of his race, had been seen moving along the crest of the mountain, and gazing down into the lovely valley which had been the favorite home of his tribe, upon the fields where he grew his corn and the sparkling stream whence he drew his fish. John used to fancy at times, as he sat there, that he could see that red spectre gliding among the trees on the hill; and if the tombstone suggested to him the trump of judgment, he could not separate it from the war-whoop that had been the last sound in the ear of Phineas Arms. The Indian always preceded murder by the war-whoop; and this was an advantage that the artillery had in the fight with the elderberry Indians. It was warned in time. If there was no war-whoop, the killing didn't count; the artilleryman got up and killed the Indian. The Indian usually had the worst of it; he not only got killed by the regulars, but he got whipped by the home-guard at night for staining himself and his clothes with the elderberry.

But once a year the company had a superlative parade. This was when the military company from the north part of the town joined the villagers in a general muster. This was an infantry company, and not to be compared with that of the village in point of evolutions. There was a great and natural hatred between the north town boys and the centre. I don't know why, but no contiguous African tribes could be more hostile. It was all right for one of either section to "lick" the other if he could, or for half a dozen to "lick" one of the enemy if they caught him alone. The notion of honor, as of mercy, comes into the boy only when he is pretty well grown; to some, neither ever comes. And yet there was an artificial military courtesy (something like that existing in the feudal age, no doubt) which put the meeting of these two rival and mutually detested companies on a high plane of behavior. It was beautiful to see the seriousness of this lofty and studied condescension on both sides. For the time, everything was under martial law. The village company being the senior, its captain commanded the united battalion in the march, and this put John temporarily into the position of captain, with the right to march at the head and "holler;" a responsibility which realized all his hopes of glory.

I suppose there has yet been discovered by man no gratification like that of marching at the head of a column in uniform on parade,—unless perhaps it is marching at their head when they are leaving a field of battle. John experienced all the thrill of this conspicuous authority, and I dare say that nothing in his later life has so exalted him in his own esteem; certainly nothing has since happened that was so important as the events of that parade day seemed. He satiated himself with all the delights of war.

# XVIII

## COUNTRY SCENES

I⊤ is impossible to say at what age a New England country boy becomes conscious that his trousers-legs are too short, and is anxious about the part of his hair and the fit of his woman-made roundabout. These harrowing thoughts come to him later than to the city lad. At least, a generation ago he served a long apprenticeship with nature only for a master, absolutely unconscious of the artificialities of life.

But I do not think his early education was neglected. And yet it is easy to underestimate the influences that, unconsciously to him, were expanding his mind and nursing in him heroic purposes. There was the lovely but narrow valley, with its rapid mountain stream; there were the great hills which he climbed only to see other hills stretching away to a broken and tempting horizon; there were the rocky pastures, and the wide sweeps of forest through which the winter tempests howled, upon which hung the haze of summer heat, over which the great shadows of summer clouds traveled; there were the clouds themselves, shouldering up above the peaks, hurrying across the narrow sky,—the clouds out of which the wind came, and the lightning and the sudden dashes of rain; and there were days when the sky was ineffably blue and distant, a fathomless vault of heaven where the hen-hawk and the eagle poised on outstretched wings and watched for their prey. Can you say how these things fed the imagination of the boy, who had few books and no contact with the great world? Do you think any city lad could have written "Thanatopsis" at eighteen?

**SLIPPERY WORK**

If you had seen John, in his short and roomy trousers and ill-used straw hat, picking his barefooted way over the rocks along the river-bank of a cool morning to see if an eel had "got on," you would not have fancied that he lived in an ideal world. Nor did he consciously. So far as he knew, he had no more sentiment than a jack-knife. Although he loved Cynthia Rudd devotedly, and blushed scarlet one day when his cousin found a lock of Cynthia's flaming hair in the box where John kept his fish-hooks, spruce gum, flag-root, tickets of standing at the head, gimlet, billets-doux in blue ink, a vile liquid in a bottle to make fish bite, and other precious possessions, yet Cynthia's society had no attractions for him comparable to a day's trout-fishing. She was, after all, only a single and a very undefined item in his general ideal world, and there was no harm in letting his imagination play about her illumined head. Since Cynthia had "got religion" and John had got nothing, his love was tempered with a little awe and a feeling of distance. He was not fickle, and yet I cannot say that he was not ready to construct a new romance in which Cynthia should be eliminated. Nothing was easier. Perhaps it was a luxurious traveling-carriage, drawn by two splendid horses in plated harness, driven along the sandy road. There were a gentleman and a young lad on the front seat, and on the back seat a handsome, pale lady with a little girl beside her. Behind, on the rack with the trunk, was a colored boy, an imp out of a story-book. John was told that the black boy was a slave, and that the carriage was from Baltimore. Here was a chance for a romance. Slavery, beauty, wealth, haughtiness, especially on the part of the slender boy on the front seat,—here was an opening into a vast realm. The high-stepping horses and the shining harness were enough to excite John's admiration, but these were nothing to the little girl. His eyes had never before fallen upon that kind of girl; he had hardly imagined that such a lovely creature could exist. Was it the soft and dainty toilet, was it the brown curls, or the large laughing eyes, or the delicate, finely cut features, or the charming little figure of this fairy-like person? Was this expression on her mobile face merely that of amusement at seeing a country boy? Then John hated her. On the contrary, did she see in him what John felt himself to be? Then he would go the world over to serve her. In a moment he was self-conscious. His trousers seemed to creep higher up his legs, and he could feel his very ankles blush. He hoped that she had not seen the other side of him, for in fact the patches were not of the exact shade of the rest of the cloth. The vision flashed by him in a moment, but it left him with a resentful feeling. Perhaps that proud little girl would be sorry some day, when he had become a general, or written a book, or kept a store, to see him go away and marry another. He almost made up his cruel mind on the instant that he would never marry her, however bad she might feel. And yet he couldn't get her out of his mind for days and days, and when her image was present even Cynthia in the singers' seat on Sunday looked a little cheap and common. Poor Cynthia! Long before John became a general, or had his revenge on the Baltimore girl, she married a farmer and was the mother of children, red-headed; and when John saw her years after, she looked tired and discouraged, as one who has carried into womanhood none of the romance of her youth.

Fishing and dreaming, I think, were the best amusements John had. The middle pier of the long covered bridge over the river stood upon a great rock, and this rock (which was known as the swimming-rock, whence the boys on summer evenings dived into the deep pool by its side) was a favorite spot with John when he could get an hour or two from the everlasting "chores." Making his way out to it over the rocks at low water with his fish-pole, there he was content to sit and observe the world; and there he saw a great deal of life. He always expected to catch the legendary trout which weighed two pounds and was believed to inhabit that pool. He always did catch horned dace and shiners, which he despised, and sometimes he snared a monstrous sucker a foot and a half long. But in the summer the sucker is a flabby fish, and John was not thanked for bringing him home. He liked, however, to lie with his face close to the water and watch the long fishes panting in the clear depths, and occasionally he would drop a pebble near one to see how gracefully he would scud away with one wave of the tail into deeper water. Nothing fears the little brown boy. The yellow-bird slants his wings, almost touches the deep water before him, and then escapes away under the bridge to the east with a glint of sunshine on his back; the fish-hawk comes down with a swoop, dips one wing, and, his prey having darted under a stone, is away again over the still hill, high soaring on even-poised pinions, keeping an eye perhaps upon the great eagle which is sweeping the sky in widening circles.

**RIGGING UP THE FISHING TACKLE**

But there is other life. A wagon rumbles over the bridge, and the farmer and his wife, jogging along, do not know that they have startled a lazy boy into a momentary fancy that a thunder-shower is coming up. John can see, as he lies there on a still summer day with the fishes and the birds for company, the road that comes down the left bank of the river, a hot, sandy, well-traveled road, hidden from view here and there by trees and bushes. The chief point of interest, however, is an enormous sycamore-tree by the roadside and in front of John's house. The house is more than a century old, and its timbers were hewed and squared by Captain Moses Rice (who lies in his grave on the hillside above it), in the presence of the Red Man who killed him with arrow and tomahawk some time after his house was set in order. The gigantic tree, struck with a sort of leprosy, like all its species, appears much older, and of course has its tradition. They say it grew from a green stake which the first land-surveyor planted there for one of his points of sight. John was reminded of it years after when he sat under the shade of the decrepit lime-tree in Freiberg and was told that it was originally a twig which the breathless and bloody messenger carried in his hand when he dropped exhausted in the square with the word "Victory!" on his lips, announcing thus the result of the glorious battle of Morat, where the Swiss in 1476 defeated Charles the Bold. Under the broad but scanty shade of the great button-ball tree (as it was called) stood an old watering-trough, with its half-decayed penstock and well-worn spout pouring forever cold sparkling water into the overflowing trough. It is fed by a spring near by, and the water is sweeter and colder than any in the known world, unless it be the well Zem-Zem, as generations of people and horses which have drunk of it would testify if they could come back. And if they could file along this road again, what a procession there would be riding down the valley!—antiquated vehicles, rusty wagons adorned with the invariable buffalo-robe even in the hottest days, lean and long-favored horses, frisky colts, drawing generation after generation the sober and pious saints that passed this way to meeting and to mill.

What a refreshment is that water-spout! All day long there are pilgrims to it, and John likes nothing better than to watch them. Here comes a gray horse drawing a buggy with two men,—cattle-buyers probably. Out jumps a man, down goes the check-rein. What a good draught the nag takes! Here comes a long-stepping trotter in a sulky; man in a brown linen coat and wide-awake hat,—dissolute, horsey-looking man. They turn up, of course. Ah! there is an establishment he knows well; a sorrel horse and an old chaise. The sorrel horse scents the water afar off, and begins to turn up long before he reaches the trough, thrusting out his nose in anticipation of the cool sensation. No check to let down; he plunges his nose in nearly to his eyes in his haste to get at it. Two maiden ladies—unmistakably such, though they appear neither "anxious nor aimless"—within the scoop-top smile benevolently on the sorrel back. It is the deacon's horse, a meeting-going nag, with a sedate, leisurely jog as he goes; and these are two of the "salt of the earth,"—the brevet rank of the women who stand and wait,—going down to the village store to dicker. There come two men in a hurry, horse driven up smartly and pulled up short; but as it is rising ground, and the horse does not easily reach the water with the wagon pulling back, the nervous man in the buggy hitches forward on his seat, as if that would carry the wagon a little ahead! Next, lumber-wagon with load of boards; horse wants to turn up, and driver switches him and cries "G'lang," and the horse reluctantly goes by, turning his head wistfully towards the flowing spout. Ah! here comes an equipage strange to these parts, and John stands up to look: an elegant carriage and two horses; trunks strapped on behind; gentleman and boy on front seat and two ladies on back seat,—city people. The gentleman descends, unchecks the horses, wipes his brow, takes a drink at the spout and looks around, evidently remarking upon the lovely view, as he swings his handkerchief in an explanatory manner. Judicious travelers! John would like to know who they are. Perhaps they are from Boston, whence come all the wonderfully painted peddlers' wagons drawn by six stalwart horses, which the driver, using no rein, controls with his long whip and cheery voice. If so, great is the condescension of Boston; and John follows them with an undefined longing as they drive away toward the mountains of Zoar. Here is a footman, dusty and tired, who comes with lagging steps. He stops, removes his hat, as he should to such a tree, puts his mouth to the spout, and takes a long pull at the lively water. And then he goes on, perhaps to Zoar, perhaps to a worse place.

**WATCHING THE FISHES**

So they come and go all the summer afternoon; but the great event of the day is the passing down the valley of the majestic stage-coach, the vast yellow-bodied, rattling vehicle. John can hear a mile off the shaking of chains, traces, and whiffle-trees, and the creaking of its leathern braces, as the great bulk swings along piled high with trunks. It represents to John, somehow, authority, government, the right of way; the driver is an autocrat,—everybody must make way for the stage-coach. It almost satisfies the imagination, this royal vehicle; one can go in it to the confines of the world,—to Boston and to Albany.

There were other influences that I dare say contributed to the boy's education. I think his imagination was stimulated by a band of gypsies who used to come every summer and pitch a tent on a little roadside patch of green turf by the river-bank, not far from his house. It was shaded by elms and butternut-trees, and a long spit of sand and pebbles ran out from it into the brawling stream. Probably they were not a very good kind of gypsy, although the story was that the men drank and beat the women. John didn't know much about drinking; his experience of it was confined to sweet cider; yet he had already set himself up as a reformer, and joined the Cold Water Band. The object of this Band was to walk in a procession under a banner that declared,—

> "So here we pledge perpetual hate
> To all that can intoxicate;"

and wear a badge with this legend, and above it the device of a well-curb with a long sweep. It kept John and all the little boys and girls from being drunkards till they were ten or eleven years of age; though perhaps a few of them died meantime from eating loaf-cake and pie and drinking ice-cold water at the celebrations of the Band.

The gypsy camp had a strange fascination for John, mingled of curiosity and fear. Nothing more alien could come into the New England life than this tatterdemalion band. It was hardly credible that here were actually people who lived outdoors, who slept in their covered wagon or under their tent, and cooked in the open air; it was a visible romance transferred from foreign lands and the remote times of the story-books; and John took these city thieves, who were on their annual foray into the country, trading and stealing horses and robbing hen-roosts and cornfields, for the mysterious race who for thousands of years have done these same things in all lands, by right of their pure blood and ancient lineage. John was afraid to approach the camp when any of the scowling and villanous men were lounging about, pipes in mouth; but he took more courage when only women and children were visible. The swarthy, black-haired women in dirty calico frocks were anything but attractive, but they spoke softly to the boy, and told his fortune, and wheedled him into bringing them any amount of cucumbers and green corn in the course of the season. In front of the tent were planted in the ground three poles that met together at the top, whence depended a kettle. This was the kitchen, and it was sufficient. The fuel for the fire was the driftwood of the stream. John noted that it did not require to be sawed into stove-lengths; and, in short, that the "chores" about this establishment were reduced to the minimum. And an older person than John might envy the free life of these wanderers, who paid neither rent nor taxes, and yet enjoyed all the delights of nature. It seemed to the boy that affairs would go more smoothly in the world if everybody would live in this simple manner. Nor did he then know, or ever after find out, why it is that the world only permits wicked people to be Bohemians.

ENTERING THE OLD BRIDGE

# XIX

## A CONTRAST TO THE NEW ENGLAND BOY

One evening at vespers in Genoa, attracted by a burst of music from the swinging curtain of the doorway, I entered a little church much frequented by the common people. An unexpected and exceedingly pretty sight rewarded me.

It was All-Souls' Day. In Italy almost every day is set apart for some festival, or belongs to some saint or another; and I suppose that when leap-year brings around the extra day, there is a saint ready to claim the 29th of February. Whatever the day was to the elders, the evening was devoted to the children. The first thing I noticed was, that the quaint old church was lighted up with innumerable wax-tapers,—an uncommon sight, for the darkness of a Catholic church in the evening is usually relieved only by a candle here and there, and by a blazing pyramid of them on the high altar. The use of gas is held to be a vulgar thing all over Europe, and especially unfit for a church or an aristocratic palace.

Then I saw that each taper belonged to a little boy or girl, and the groups of children were scattered all about the church. There was a group by every side altar and chapel, all the benches were occupied by knots of them, and there were so many circles of them seated on the pavement that I could with difficulty make my way among them. There were hundreds of children in the church, all dressed in their holiday apparel, and all intent upon the illumination, which seemed to be a private affair to each one of them.

And not much effect had their tapers upon the darkness of the vast vaults above them. The tapers were little spiral coils of wax, which the children unrolled as fast as they burned, and when they were tired of holding them they rested them on the ground and watched the burning. I stood some time by a group of a dozen seated in a corner of the church. They had massed all the tapers in the centre and formed a ring about the spectacle, sitting with their legs straight out before them and their toes turned up. The light shone full in their happy faces, and made the group, enveloped otherwise in darkness, like one of Correggio's pictures of children or angels. Correggio was a famous Italian artist of the sixteenth century, who painted cherubs like children who were just going to heaven, and children like cherubs who had just come out of it. But then, he had the Italian children for models, and they get the knack of being lovely very young. An Italian child finds it as easy to be pretty as an American child to be good.

**THE OLD WATERING TROUGH**

One could not but be struck with the patience these little people exhibited in their occupation, and the enjoyment they got out of it. There was no noise; all conversed in subdued whispers and behaved in the most gentle manner to each other, especially to the smallest, and there were many of them so small that they could only toddle about by the most judicious exercise of their equilibrium. I do not say this by way of reproof to any other kind of children.

These little groups, as I have said, were scattered all about the church; and they made with their tapers little spots of light, which looked in the distance very much like Correggio's picture which is at Dresden,—the Holy Family at Night, and the light from the Divine Child blazing in the faces of all the attendants. Some of the children were infants in the nurse's arms, but no one was too small to have a taper, and to run the risk of burning its fingers.

There is nothing that a baby likes more than a lighted candle, and the church has understood this longing in human nature, and found means to gratify it by this festival of tapers.

The groups do not all remain long in place, you may imagine; there is a good deal of shifting about, and I see little stragglers wandering over the church, like fairies lighted by fire-flies. Occasionally they form a little procession and march from one altar to another, the lights twinkling as they go.

But all this time there is music pouring out of the organ-loft at the end of the church, and flooding all its spaces with its volume. In front of the organ is a choir of boys, led by a round-faced and jolly monk, who rolls about as he sings, and lets the deep bass noise rumble about a long time in his stomach before he pours it out of his mouth. I can see the faces of all of them quite well, for each singer has a candle to light his music-book.

And next to the monk stands the boy,—the handsomest boy in the whole world probably at this moment. I can see now his great, liquid, dark eyes and his exquisite face, and the way he tossed back his long waving hair when he struck into his part. He resembled the portraits of Raphael, when that artist was a boy; only I think he looked better than Raphael, and without trying, for he seemed to be a spontaneous sort of boy. And how that boy did sing! He was the soprano of the choir, and he had a voice of heavenly sweetness. When he opened his mouth and tossed back his head, he filled the church with exquisite melody.

He sang like a lark, or like an angel. As we never heard an angel sing, that comparison is not worth much. I have seen pictures of angels singing,—there is one by Jan and Hubert Van Eyck in the gallery at Berlin,—and they open their mouths like this boy, but I can't say as much for their singing. The lark, which you very likely never heard either,—for larks are as scarce in America as angels,—is a bird that springs up from the meadow and begins to sing as he rises in a spiral flight, and the higher he mounts the sweeter he sings, until you think the notes are dropping out of heaven itself, and you hear him when he is gone from sight, and you think you hear him long after all sound has ceased.

And yet this boy sang better than a lark, because he had more notes and a greater compass and more volume, although he shook out his voice in the same gleesome abundance.

I am sorry that I cannot add that this ravishingly beautiful boy was a good boy. He was probably one of the most mischievous boys that was ever in an organ-loft. All time that he was singing the vespers he was skylarking like an imp. While he was pouring out the most divine melody, he would take the opportunity of kicking the shins of the boy next to him; and while he was waiting for his part he would kick out behind at any one who was incautious enough to approach him.

There never was such a vicious boy; he kept the whole loft in a ferment. When the monk rumbled his bass in his stomach, the boy cut up monkey-shines that set every other boy into a laugh, or he stirred up a row that set them all at fisticuffs.

**THE NEW ENGLAND BOY**

And yet this boy was a great favorite. The jolly monk loved him best of all, and bore with his wildest pranks. When he was wanted to sing his part and was sky-larking in the rear, the fat monk took him by the ear and brought him forward; and when he gave the boy's ear a twist, the boy opened his lovely mouth and poured forth such a flood of melody as you never heard. And he didn't mind his notes; he seemed to know his notes by heart, and could sing and look off like a nightingale on a bough. He knew his power, that boy; and he stepped forward to his stand when he pleased, certain that he would be forgiven as soon as he began to sing. And such spirit and life as he threw into the performance, rollicking through the Vespers with a perfect abandon of carriage, as if he could sing himself out of his skin if he liked!

While the little angels down below were pattering about with their wax tapers, keeping the holy fire burning, suddenly the organ stopped, the monk shut his book with a bang, the boys blew out the candles, and I heard them all tumbling down stairs in a gale of noise and laughter. The beautiful boy I saw no more.

About him plays the light of tender memory; but were he twice as lovely, I could never think of him as having either the simple manliness or the good fortune of the New England boy.

Lector House believes that a society develops through a two-fold approach of continuous learning and adaptation, which is derived from the study of classic literary works spread across the historic timeline of literature records. Therefore, we aim at reviving, repairing and redeveloping all those inaccessible or damaged but historically as well as culturally important literature across subjects so that the future generations may have an opportunity to study and learn from past works to embark upon a journey of creating a better future.

This book is a result of an effort made by Lector House towards making a contribution to the preservation and repair of original ancient works which might hold historical significance to the approach of continuous learning across subjects.

**HAPPY READING & LEARNING!**

LECTOR HOUSE LLP
E-MAIL: lectorpublishing@gmail.com

9 789390 314201